TO
HEAL
AND
TO
REVEAL

TO
HEAL
AND
TO
REVEAL

The Prophetic
Vocation
According to Luke

PAUL S. MINEAR

A CROSSROAD BOOK
THE SEABURY PRESS
NEW YORK

THE SEABURY PRESS
815 Second Avenue
New York, N.Y. 10017

Printed in the United States of America

Library of Congress Cataloging in Publication Data

Minear, Paul Sevier, 1906–
    To heal and to reveal.

    "A Crossroad book."
    Includes index.
1. Prophecy (Christianity)—Biblical teaching—Addresses, essays, lectures. 2. Gifts,
Spiritual—Biblical teaching—Addresses, essays, lectures. 3. Bible. N.T. Luke—Criticism,
interpretation, etc.—Addresses, essays, lectures. I. Title.
BS2545.P72M56   226'.4'015   75-42213   ISBN 0-8164-0295-7

CONTENTS

PREFACE

PART ONE of this book represents lectures that were given first at Providence College and then at Princeton Theological Seminary during the summer of 1973. I here record my gratitude to my hosts on those occasions, especially to Father Mark Heath, O.P., and Father James J. Davis, O.P., at Providence, and to President James I. McCord and his able staff at Princeton. Part Two constitutes the substance of the Shaffer Lectures, given at Yale Divinity School, February 19–21, 1974. It is quite beyond my power to express the depth of appreciation to my former colleagues for the honor of this invitation and the warmth of their welcome. Chapters 4 through 6 were used again during the summer of 1974 in the Biblical Institute at Trinity College, Burlington, Vermont, under the gracious supervision of Sister Miriam Ward.

The publication of this book marks the completion of four decades of writing in the field of biblical interpretation. During that entire period, virtually every essay and chapter has profited beyond measure from the perceptive comments and penetrating criticisms of my wife. If there were full justice in such matters, she would have appeared on every title page as joint author. Let that fact now be gratefully acknowledged!

Part One

THE PROPHETIC LANGUAGE

1

The only way forward is to repudiate our contemporary "flat-earthers" —the thinkers who reduce every vertical to a horizontal, all language to the literal meaning of words, all relation with God to a relation with men. [1]

THE SOURCE OF AUTHORITY

IT MAY HAVE BEEN TRUE, once upon a time, that study of the Bible made students more aware of the nearness of their own world to the ancient world of biblical authors. It was then quite possible to visualize the movement of the intervening time as a smoothly flowing river linking the modern world to the ancient, and enhancing the frequency of communication. But that time has long since vanished. The river of the centuries now makes us aware of our isolation from that ancient world. The torrent flows so rapidly, it tumbles over so many waterfalls, it passes through such grotesque panoramas, that we now find it extremely difficult to make our way against the stream into that ancient world. Modern education, not least in the theological seminary, has made us all aliens in the world of the Bible, and the men of the Bible aliens in our world. This is why an effective study of the Bible produces culture shock; the more intense the study, the greater the shock.

To be sure, we can all find ways to minimize this shock. Like Americans junketing in Asia, we can carefully select the itinerary, stop only at Western-style hotels, use guides who speak fluent English, eat only American food, albeit with quaint seasonings, and

3

shop for foreign bric-a-brac with Bankamericards. Indeed the guiding of travelers through the world of the Bible with a minimum of culture shock is often assumed to be the chief function of ministers and teachers. They are expected to limit the questions and to select the answers which will not threaten the self-assurance of their customers. They are duty-bound to translate words or ideas, one at a time, into contemporary American jargon and ideology, so that any emotional disturbance will be minimized. They preserve the illusion of travel, without its risk or its profit. They remain blissfully unaware of how completely they have destroyed the integrity and independence of that other world.

But past shock can be as devastating as future shock. To achieve a genuine penetration of the ancient world can actually destroy a person's at-homeness in his own habitat. In fact we cannot fully grasp the cogency of ancient ways of thinking without surrendering that habitat. In ancient literature we encounter people who are marching to the sound of a different drummer; the tempo of their life is vastly different from ours. Their language is shaped by a different mentality, their mentality shaped by different experience. Their world has a different ceiling and different horizons; their maps give expression to different beginnings and endings. As long as a student shies away from that alien world, so long does Bible study remain bland, superficial, and tepid. But each step of penetration will increase his excitement, though also his bewilderment, for at each step he encounters a collision between two languages, two mentalities, two modes of existing in the world, in fact, two worlds. Each collision threatens that world in which the student has heretofore found shelter.

THE COLLISION OF TWO WORLDS

I have obviously been using the term *world* in a broad and inclusive sense to cover both visible and mental habitats, which are in fact always interlaced. The world without and the world within are one world. As Wallace Stevens has expressed it, "We live in the description of a place and not in the place itself."[2] It is the description of a place in thought and words that gives contour to the external realm of space and time, and there are an infinite number of possible descriptions for each place. The term *world* denotes both the cosmic context and the inherited, communal modes of perceiving it, both the historical process and men's modes of living within it. The term encloses both visible things and the mental map of those things, both physical environments and the humanization of those environments in mythology and science. It is as seen in this inclusive sense that I find everywhere in the Bible a collision between the two worlds, and this collision makes Bible study increasingly difficult.

For those to whom the term *world* is too confusing, a more subjective term may be preferable—the term *consciousness*. This term has the advantages and disadvantages of recent currency in *The Greening of America* by Charles Reich[3] and also in the women's liberation movement. *World* is more cosmological, *consciousness* more psychological. *Consciousness* accents the organized pattern of perceptions by which men visualize their habitat and locate their own paths within it, the maps by which they orient themselves vis-á-vis cosmic contexts, historical processes, and human communities, the biographical charts on which they locate the beginnings and endings, the purposes and momenta of the complex pilgrimage of life. In this sense I find vast distances between the consciousness of New Testament authors (hereafter to be called Consciousness B) and the various types of consciousness animating modern readers (Consciousness A). And in these chapters I will be concerned with the degree to which Consciousness B has become unintelligible to Consciousness A.

If we measure the Bible's vitality by its power to shape the world views of its readers, we are obliged to conclude that the Bible no longer lives. The crisis within the churches today is not unrelated to that death, a death which may be even more pervasive in the lives of self-assured believers than in the more honest confessions of sceptics. I am convinced that the Bible will remain moribund until Consciousness B again becomes intelligible to readers imbued with Consciousness A; and this will not happen until the implicit collisions between the two worlds become the object of deliberate study. In what follows I will try to make more intelligible certain structural components in the prophetic consciousness, stressing in Part One distinctive elements in the language, and in Part Two distinctive elements in the vocation.

The nature of this goal places three demands on our thinking, each of which carries a corresponding danger. First of all, we must try to think in terms not of separate notions but of complex constellations of attitudes as interdependent wholes. We must be able to comprehend the structural girders which give inner stability to a particular world view. The map of Consciousness B has its own polar magnetisms, its own motivational and directional grids. Before we can photograph this terrain, we must gain a certain altitude above it. As meteorologists now use satellites to photograph the clouds covering an entire continent in order to forecast tomorrow's weather in Iowa or in Maine, so biblical students need to gain a stratospheric vision of ancient landscapes of thought.

This effort to secure an overview of Consciousness B involves, however, the danger of losing the student in vast panoramas of vague generalizations. Our thoughts may become so grandiose that, to use Søren Kierkegaard's terms, we succumb to that despair which is due to an overdose of infinitude and a deficiency in finitude.[4] We would be like men trying to find their way around the streets of Copenhagen with a map of the universe in their hands. The task therefore makes a second demand, that we combine the macroscopic study of wider frames of reference with microscopic study of specific texts. We must be able to follow, point by point, the successive ideas of a particular author, locating within these ideas clues to his implicit world-scape. Should a particular idea disclose its context in Consciousness B, we must not neglect, in our concern for that context, the more immediate concern of the author with that particular idea.

Absorption in the details of his thinking may, of course, induce a form of despair opposite to the earlier one, in this case a despair produced by a surfeit of the finite and a famine of the infinite. We might be trying to explore stellar space with a map of Copenhagen in our hands. To overcome this tendency we must remember that each word derives its meaning from its own sentence, each sentence from its own paragraph, and each idea from its ultimate habitat. We show our respect for an author only by recognizing both the coherence of his thought world as a whole and the significance within that world of each specific idea.

There is a third demand, that we make judicious use of the resources of modern biblical scholarship. There are those, of course, who fear the work of scholars, believing that scholarly objectivity is incompatible with faith. It is true that one can cite examples where beliefs have crumbled before advances in knowledge, yet thousands of Christian scholars have demonstrated the fruitfulness of combining objectivity and commitment. Think what you will on that issue, we will be unable to make headway on a project such as this without building on the honest work of generations of scholars.

Even though we acknowledge this debt, we must admit that many scholars have defaulted on the task we are attempting. Although knowledge of the Bible has proliferated, the net effect has been to leave the Christian community less interested in the Bible and even less at home in it. What we have called Consciousness B has become steadily less intelligible and less accessible. Why so? In part because modern historians (and exegetes do visualize themselves primarily as historians) have been taken captive by methodologies that have been dominated by the presuppositions of Consciousness A. For instance, they often assume an attitude toward events in history which is tacitly atheistic. Consequently, in dealing with texts which speak of the convergence of divine and human forces, they limit attention to human forces alone.[5]

As another instance, current methodologies utilize post-Renaissance conceptions of the nature of chronological time and of the historical process, conceptions which do scant justice to the richness and complexity of those attitudes characteristic of Consciousness B. Earlier in this century, it was the laity in American churches who seemed most vulnerable to the "acids of modernity." More recently the clergy have proved most vulnerable, often because their historical studies have been permeated by a methodology that is inherently relativistic and agnostic.[6] This has undermined their respect for an ancient writer like Luke and has precluded any genuine appropriation of his outlook. This fact simply reinforces the third demand on those who would recover that outlook: while utilizing the resources of modern scholarship, they must seek to remain independent of its implicit world views.

To summarize our objectives: we have set our hand to the recovery of the prophetic consciousness as it is embodied in specific texts in the two-volume work of Luke. In the first instance this will require the examination of several pivotal terms in his vocabulary, following principles set forth by Paul Ricoeur:

> To understand a text is to follow its movement from sense to reference; from what it says to what it talks about. What has to be understood is not the initial situation of discourse but what points to a possible world. [The text offers us] a new way of looking at things, an injunction to think in a certain manner. The text speaks of a possible world and of a possible way of orienting oneself within it.[7]

What we have called consciousness includes these phrases of Ricoeur: a "way of looking at things," "to think in a certain manner," a "way of orienting oneself" within a world. In the case of Luke, of course, such a consciousness is indigenous to a world where God is the author of all times and seasons (Acts 1: 7). Moreover, this consciousness is a response to God's activity, to his calling of his people to orient themselves to the world of his creation and to the goals of his salvation. In other words, participation in this vocation becomes necessary to the comprehension of Luke's language, a matter to which Part Two is devoted.

EIGHT CLUES TO CONSCIOUSNESS B

We will first examine Luke 10:1–16, asking what this passage may say about a "possible world and a possible way of orienting oneself within it," seeking to chart that constellation of convictions which together give coherence and substance to Consciousness B.

The chapter tells of the commissioning of messengers by Jesus for a mission to the cities of Galilee and Samaria. I will use my own rather free translation.

After this [i.e., after Jesus had told the crowds what it would cost them to join his pilgrimage to Jerusalem] the Lord chose and sent seventy-two [or seventy] other men to travel in pairs into every city or place into which he would come. This was his assignment:

"A large harvest is ready but there are too few harvesters. So beg God, the Lord of the harvest, to send out more harvesters. Be on your way. I am sending you like lambs into a pack of wolves, so be on your guard. You must travel light, without pocketbook, bag, or sandals. You must not stop to chat along the way. When you enter a house greet it, 'Peace to this home.' If a son of peace lives there, your peace will rest on him. If not, it will return to you. Remain in that house, taking whatever food and drink they provide, for the worker deserves wages. Don't scrounge from house to house. On arriving in a city, if its residents welcome you, eat whatever they serve. Heal the sick who are there and announce to them, 'To you the kingdom of God has come near.' But if, on arrival, the city does not welcome you, make this announcement as you leave its streets: 'This dust from your streets which has stuck to our feet we shake off. Nevertheless, don't forget, the kingdom of God has come near.' I tell you Sodom will fare better on that day than that city.

"You Chorazin, you Bethsaida, you are both damned. For if Tyre and Sidon had witnessed the signs of God's power wrought in you they would long ago have repented, in clothes made of sacking and with faces covered with ashes. On the great Judgment Day Tyre and Sidon will fare better than you. And what about you, Capernaum? You will be humiliated in Hades, not exalted to heaven.

"Anyone who offers you hospitality offers it to me, anyone who scoffs at you scoffs at me, anyone who scoffs at me scoffs at him who commissioned me."

Let us now look beyond what this text says to the Consciousness B to which it points. What are the structural convictions without which the story would lose its intelligibility? One might select many clues, but among them four seem essential to the structure of thinking, each of the four reflecting a cluster of satellite axioms.

1. A central role is accorded the activity of a particular deity, a God who is accessible through and responsive to prayer. He is the lord of this particular harvest; he alone can find and authorize harvesters, who will in turn convey announcements of his judgments and signs of his power. His active though invisible presence becomes in some sense coterminous with the journey and mission. What will happen derives its meaning from the messengers' bond to him, as well as from his purpose for the houses and the cities they will visit. What was true of the prewar Jewish ghettos of Poland, as described by Bernard Sachs, was even more true of Luke's community: "Everything soared upwards towards God—the author, producer and critic of the drama that was being enacted under the arc-light of eternity."[8]

2. The text assumes that God's kingdom has been set in motion toward these particular communities and that this movement is related to the process of harvesting. It is this movement that energizes the journey of the reapers, that becomes articulate in their message, that gives an ultimate significance to men's responses to it, whether positive or negative. This kingdom appears to matter because the future fate of these men and these cities derives from it. The decision to extend hospitality to the travelers would, in fact, mark the very incursion of that kingdom.

3. The words of Jesus imply that even before they were uttered, he had received authority to speak and to act as God's agent, with sufficient authority over the messengers to give them instructions on where to go, how to travel, and what to say. The setting seems to imply that to Luke their mission had become a segment of Jesus' own journey toward Jerusalem (9:51), a journey which held awesome meanings for him, for them, and for the redemption of Israel.

4. The text anticipates a portentous struggle between these lambs and the wolves to which they were sent, a struggle which seems an inevitable result of the impact of their message on the cities of Israel. There is something about that message that creates danger and invites derision and rejection. As an analogy for that impact, the

speaker has recourse to communal memories of Sodom, Tyre, and
Sidon.

These, then, are four axiomatic attitudes which are implicit in
this version of Consciousness B: the power-laden presence of God,
the immediate ingression of his kingdom in the situations described,
the authority of Jesus as his spokesman, and the polarization of
conflict among the residents of Israel. I make three further observations, without supporting them with argument at the moment.
Each of the four facets of the story is essential to the intelligibility of
the whole complex; the world view reflected in them is quite distinctive; none of the four can be assimilated easily into the mentality of a
modern reader, and even less can the constellation as a whole.

Now we return to Luke's text for an appraisal of other points of
collision, as reflected in his account of the return of the messengers:

> The seventy-two returned to Jesus, shouting for joy: "Lord, when in
> your authority we issue commands, even the demons obey us." Then he
> replied: "I have been watching Satan falling from heaven like lightning.
> Look here. I have issued to you the power to crush the heads of snakes
> and scorpions, power greater than any power of the Enemy, so that he
> can no longer harm you. Are you happy that the demons obey you? You
> should be even happier that your names have been inscribed in heaven."
>
> It was at that very hour that Jesus, filled with the Holy Spirit,
> exulted: "Father, you who rule heaven and earth, I give my witness that
> you have hidden what is happening from wise and educated men and
> have disclosed it to infants. That was your wise and gracious decision.
> My father has transferred all authority to me. So no one but the father
> can recognize who the son is. No one but the son can recognize who the
> father is—and those to whom the son decides to disclose him."
>
> Then privately he said to his disciples: "Blessed are the eyes which see
> what you are now seeing. I declare to you that many prophets and kings
> have wanted to see what you see, and to hear what you hear, but it was
> not granted to them" (10:17–24).

Very strange dialogue this, and hardly of a kind to be matched
anywhere in the modern world. Very mysterious, since everything

decisive is invisible or at least hidden from all except Jesus and his chosen delegates. These verses reinforce the four attitudes already discovered: the awareness of God's active presence in all that happens, the disruptive force of God's kingdom as it impinges on men's lives, the unlimited scope of authority asserted by Jesus, and the enlarging circle of conflict into which the messengers were propelled by their mission. This text enables us to note several additional convictions which must become intelligible before the thought pattern as a whole will make sense.

5. The text assumes the reality of heaven as both immediately and ultimately significant. It is the source of authority, the "space" from which Satan falls or is expelled, the "place" where the delegates' names are inscribed. The dialogue implies that heaven is "really invisible," so invisible that special eyes and ears are needed; yet it is also "invisibly real," so real as to determine what happens on earth.

6. The dialogue assumes that the Holy Spirit plays a vital role in providing contact between the invisible and the visible realms. It is the source of Jesus' power, his joy, and his knowledge; it is necessary for the communication of "knowledge" between the Father and the Son, between the Son and the "infants." It discloses to the messengers things long hidden from prophets and kings.

7. Readers can now understand that the conflict between lambs and wolves, as noted above, is simply one phase of a wider warfare, the continuing struggle between God and Satan, between Jesus and the demons, a struggle in which a specific defeat of Satan in heaven precedes the earthly warfare in which the seventy-two are engaged, and enables them to fight.

8. Various functions of those delegates become clearer. They are not only agents in the expulsion of demons (with accompanying reverberations in human life) and healers of the sick; they also reveal heavenly knowledge that has long been hidden. They have learned who the Son is and, through him, who the Father is. They continue the work of prophets and kings; their work represents a miraculous culmination of the work of earlier revealers and rulers. Signs and

wonders of various kinds attend the collision between the two realms and portend astonishing victories over all the powers of "the Enemy."

It would be possible to select other convictions that are important in the overall structure, but these four adequately indicate the scope and complexity of the problem: the strategic and pervasive references to heaven, the hidden but no less decisive activity of the Holy Spirit, the dramatic battle with Satan and his cohorts, and the gift of miraculous powers and knowledge to these specific prophets and kings. When we add these to the first four axioms we can begin to grasp the depth of the difficulties that stand between us and full comprehension of that mode of existence to which the text points. These skeletal girders of thought are as foreign to consciousness A as they are native to consciousness B. No task can be more subtle and more complex than that of making this thought world fully intelligible to men whose instinctive pictures of reality have been shaped by consciousness A. This is *the* problem of biblical interpretation today.

If I may make a short detour, let me here address a comment to my exegetical colleagues. I am convinced that we have devoted too little of our time and wisdom to this problem. Too often we have tried to shift responsibility to other shoulders. One familiar evasion utilizes a map on which two separate routes are marked: the historical method of approach as separate from the devotional, "as though mental integrity and moral affinity could only thrive apart in the quest for a real Jesus." I am happy to associate myself on this matter with one of the earliest Shaffer lecturers, with James Moffatt, who wrote "Such a notion belongs to prejudices of the street and the study which are no longer tenable."[9] Those prejudices are no longer tenable because this matter of recovering the world view of the ancient writer is a matter of prime concern not only to the believer but to the historian as well.

A second evasion utilizes a provincial academic map in which a vast mountain range separates the historical disciplines from the theological, a map wherein the cartographers contend that it is the work of the theologian to deal with the problem of meanings but that this work must be postponed until after the historian has described with due objectivity the course and character of biblical history. Again I contend that this evasion is no longer defensible. The target of study itself (the dimensions and ramifications of consciousness B) antedates the artificial separations of the historical from the theological and thus requires the student to transcend those separations if he is to comprehend the ancient thought patterns. Luke's view of the "historical" events is such that the historian cannot fully comprehend that view so long as he postpones to a later date or assigns to another technician the task of assessing the "theological" data. The project in which we are engaged is a primary responsibility of the historian even though the texts themselves force him to deal with data that do not conform to the mesh of the sieves which he is in the habit of using. Whether or not this protest is deemed cogent, I insist that the task undertaken in this volume must be viewed not as something optional for the historian, though necessary for the minister or theologian, but as something inescapable for every interpreter of Scripture, whatever may be his professional niche.

Returning to the eight basic clues to Luke's version of Consciousness B, we may now ask where we may find an auspicious place to begin our study. At what point can we best take hold of the problem in which all clues appear to be alien to the mentality, let us say, of readers of the *New York Times* or the *Congressional Record*? We might well begin with an analysis of Luke's frequent references to heaven. These references surely provide an essential context for his thinking, yet just as surely they provide obstacles to the modern reader's comprehension. The word *heaven* projects on the screen of our minds a geographical region appearing on the map of the stellar universe. In view of prevailing scientific knowledge, such a projection strikes us as ridiculous, and accordingly we have virtually ceased to use the word to express any deeper thoughts of our own. To rehabilitate the term for serious use would seem to require intellectual dishonesty. At the very least, the term fails to convey the meanings that it held for Luke.

Or we might well begin with the task of making Luke's views of the miraculous more convincing. In some respects the early Christian appeals to signs and wonders are least credible of all the New Testament ideas. Such things simply do not happen. Those who accept Luke's stories at face value and who make them the basis of faith become easy targets for the scorn of tough-minded realists. It is quite impossible to protect Luke himself from this scorn, since not only are his pages sprinkled with fabulous stories, but his basic orientation seems to require the acceptance of such stories (e.g., the narratives of birth and resurrection). Some resolution of this clash between ancient and modern attitudes toward the miraculous must precede full comprehension.

Yet instead of starting with one of these two riddles, I have chosen to start with another cluster of ideas where the chasm between Luke's thinking and our own is not so deep and where, as a consequence, it may be easier to throw a rope-bridge over the ravine. I believe that if we examine Luke's attitudes toward diverse kinds of authority and how each is exercised, we may find sufficient congruence to our own experience and thought world to disclose points of contact. Progress toward making this cluster intelligible may then contribute to greater comprehension of the others and may even help to rehabilitate the Lucan references to heaven and to miracle. This, at least, is the experiment which we will make in subsequent chapters.

Let our intention be clearly understood. Our purpose is not to translate separate biblical words into words which are already familiar in our own vocabulary, giving us the illusion of comprehension. Nor is the goal the conversion of readers to a specific form of biblical faith or conduct, although we do not try to conceal our own preferences. In this study we are concerned to test the possibility of making intelligible the biblical mentality as a whole. We have chosen Luke's record at this point simply in order to safeguard the integrity of one man's thought. We do not contend that his is the best type of biblical thinking, nor is it the easiest to comprehend. In selecting it we assert only that his mode of thinking was sufficiently typical so that penetration into his mind-set should enhance efforts to comprehend what others were thinking and saying.

AUTHORITY AND AUTHORITIES

An auspicious place to start is Luke's story—a story presumably derived from a source common to him and to Matthew—of an anonymous army officer whom we may for convenience call Captain Jones (7:1–10; Mt. 8:5–13). Luke places this story quite early in the ministry of Jesus, immediately after references to the activity of Jesus in healing (6:19) and teaching the crowds of Jewish folk. As the story unfolds we learn that Captain Jones had a favorite slave who had become desperately ill. Although at the end of the story the slave is presumed to have been healed by a word from Jesus spoken at a distance, the climax of the story is to be found not in the healing but in Jesus' declaration to the Jewish crowds that Captain Jones had showed faith greater than any in Israel. This commendation (and implicit condemnation) is the real point of the story. So we are invited to ask: on what evidence did Jesus base this judgment of Captain Jones? What made his faith so great? Was it the fact that this man, though a Gentile, had developed such love for Israel that he paid for the construction of a synagogue in Capernaum? Though this devotion aroused high praise from Jewish elders, it is obvious that this was not the decisive factor for either Jesus or Luke. A second possible index of Jones's faith was provided by the message which his couriers brought even before Jesus came near the captain's house. According to this message, Jones had recognized that his home was unworthy to receive Jesus and that a command spoken from afar would be sufficient to heal the slave. Such humility and such confidence were surely signs of great faith. Yet the story puts even greater weight on another sign. In his message Jones made a statement which elicited Jesus' commendation:

"For I also am a man set under authority, with soldiers under me: and I say to one, 'Go,' and he goes; and to another, 'Come,' and he comes; and to my slave, 'Do this,' and he does it" (7:8).

Behind this statement there is more than meets the casual eye.

1. Captain Jones exercised authority over his soldiers and over his slave. By their obedience to his commands they recognized the strength of that authority. The story weaves his authority and their obedience into a single pattern which defined the relative status of both.

2. Captain Jones could exercise authority *over* them only because he stood *under* the authority of his superior, presumably the military government in the case of the soldiers and the common or civil law in the case of his slave. His right to command his inferiors was based on his duty to obey his own superiors. Any rung on the ladder presupposed the existence of the entire ladder.

3. The text assumes that what was true for Captain Jones is true for all men in positions of authority. Whatever one's status in the hierarchy, each man has a duty to obey those above him and a right to command those beneath him. Every exercise of authority discloses this hidden ladder of duty and rights.

4. Captain Jones had discerned in Jesus the existence of such a hidden ladder. In some respects Jones's and Jesus' authority were similar ("for I also," "for I myself"), that is, it was because Jesus was set under authority that he could command obedience. In other respects Jesus' authority was unique. His command was effective, not only over men but over illness, over the death that was latent in illness, and over the demons which caused the sickness. His authority as a prophet-healer had come directly from God and not from another man.

5. Jones's recognition of this comparable ladder explains the other elements in the story. Jones had felt unworthy, not simply because he was a Gentile confronting a Jew, nor a man of violence confronting a man of peace; he was a man with one kind and degree of authority confronting a man with another kind and degree. His reti-

cence underscored the disparity between the two command structures: the Roman army versus God's delegate.

6. The captain recognized several basic constituents in Jesus' authority. It could overcome the barrier of space, since he could command from a distance and be obeyed. It could overcome the barrier of death, for the slave had been at death's door. (The story which follows tells how Jesus had indeed overcome the death of a widow's son.) The powers of evil recognized their master in such a way as to cancel normal considerations of space, time, and social status.

7. We should not overlook the fact that Jones's faith in Jesus was linked to his concern for his slave. An emergency had induced this officer to give priority to the needs of his subordinate. Love had taken priority over the usual social conventions which less generous persons treat as iron laws. Jones's request of help for this slave had expressed an inner victory over self-concern.

8. The story also raises this question: why had Israel proved so lacking in this faith? The answer is not given, except in what might be inferred from the Gospel as a whole. Had Israel become in large degree immune to the message of the prophets (e.g., John and Jesus) because it had accepted the authority of the scribes, thus substituting for the immediacy of God's revelation the conventionally mediated knowledge of the scriptures? Was it because their appeal to a secondary and derived authority seemed to them so adequate that they could hear but not obey Jesus' demands (6:49)?

"Such faith I have not found, even in Israel." That statement implies at the least that Israel was the place where such faith should have been found. Instead it was a Gentile who exhibited faith by recognizing the authority of Jesus over illness and death. Captain Jones's own involvement in a military bureaucracy had enabled him to discern within a quite different bureaucracy the presence of less visible but even more significant structures of authority, and his love for his servant had encouraged him to trust those other structures. His faith was nothing less than his perception of this reality as a whole.

THE REVERSAL OF DIRECTIONS

The story of Captain Jones stressed the similarity between the two ladders of authority. In another story Luke stressed the disparity. Those who wish to catch Luke's understanding of this disparity must study carefully the dialogue which he locates at the Last Supper (22:24–30).[10] Luke here reports a dispute among the twelve apostles over which of them would be greatest. In Luke's day, of course, the apostles had become authority figures for Christians, and the question of greatness was actually the question of which apostle should be accorded authority over the others. Luke chose a setting in which Jesus' own action (at table, in Gethsemane, in the Judgment Hall, and on the cross) would serve both to dramatize the issue and to provide its resolution. The Passover/Eucharistic setting accented Jesus' refusal to eat with the Twelve until he had suffered (22:15f.)* but it also showed his readiness to eat with them after his suffering (24:30) when he could convey to them the meaning of that suffering. At the Supper itself Jesus analyzed the dispute by drawing a sharp antithesis: all exercise of authority is grounded on one of two opposite principles.

> PRINCIPLE A: "Gentile kings exercise sovereignty over Gentiles; their men of power are praised as philanthropists."

So obvious is this principle, so universal its observance, that no explication is needed. Every society and every form of human association, whether small or great, illustrates this principle. It is difficult to imagine any situation, any society, in which the infrastructure of daily life is not based upon it. This is no moralistic tirade against human sins, but rather a hard-nosed description of things as they operate in all societies at all times.

---

*Readers are so accustomed to the notion of Jesus eating with his disciples that they overlook the plain meaning of the Lucan text.

Nevertheless, as the teacher of the apostles, Jesus made mandatory for them a reverse principle:

PRINCIPLE B: "The younger must become the greater; the servant must become the ruler."

Here again there is not the slightest ambiguity. We are dealing not with pious sentimentality or with glib moralizing, but with a penetrating diagram of social realities. In this new community greater power and prestige must be accorded to those on the lower rungs of the ladder. The directional flow of societal power must be reversed. As the key to the new organizational chart, the apostles are commanded to replace Principle A with Principle B. The more universally accepted the former had been, the more revolutionary would be the adoption of the latter. So great a revolution required justification, or at least the application of an authority compelling enough to produce obedience. Yet this new authority must operate in line with the new principle. The story makes clear how Jesus had met this requirement:

PRINCIPLE A: "At a meal, which man has the higher rank, the host or the waiter? The host, of course."
PRINCIPLE B: "I am among you as the waiter."

In the earlier verses Principle A had been illustrated from the realms of political power and national prestige. Now the illustration was drawn from everyday social behavior, the status of a dinner host and his waiters. The three illustrations served to cover the entire range of societal organization: political, economic, and social. So, too, the illustrations of Principle B covered an equally wide range of differences in echelons of power, whether due to age, to wealth, or to social convention. Jesus' simple affirmation "But I" takes for granted his right to command. It assumes that this command had become binding on the apostles. Only by obeying it could they acknowledge his authority. In this way the measure of their obedience to Principle B automatically became the measure of their respect for him. He had issued his command from a lower position; it was his example, his own enactment of Principle B, that had established the norm for them. His action had become his command; by that action he had reversed the directional flow of authority. This revolution in the exercise of all forms of authority had been clinched by the picture of Jesus standing in the midst of his apostles ("I am among you"), not only at the Last Supper but in every Eucharist that would be celebrated in Luke's church.

The story of the Passover impelled Luke's readers to ponder the contrasts between the authority which operates downward from those in higher echelons and that which emanates upward from those in lower echelons. Everyone has indeed experienced both types of pressure, though the direction from which it comes determines the qualitative character of the pressure. It is in fact quite possible that Luke had been reminded of an earlier analogy, the story of Joseph and his brothers, for the twelve patriarchs are the prototypes of the twelve apostles. It had been the vision of the elder brothers bowing down to the younger that had aroused fratricidal hatred of Joseph (Gen. 37), but in spite of their attempted homicide, the younger had proved to be their salvation (Gen. 45).

That very hatred bespeaks customary attitudes toward authority among Jews as among all other societies. Certainly in Hebrew society it was assumed that elder sons, acting in the name of their father, held not only the right to rule their younger brothers but also to require respect from them (Testament of Joseph 10:6; 17:1). For the younger to be accorded the higher status constituted a revolution, a direct challenge against the legitimacy of all power structures, a challenge which Jesus asserted represented the power of God himself. The very analogies chosen by Jesus in Luke 22:25−28 disclose his intent to extend this revolution to every echelon of societal organization.[11]

By Luke's day the apostles themselves, using authority derived from this man who had taken the apron of a waiter, had become the primary source of authority for his followers. Jesus' prophecy had been fulfilled, in accordance with Principle B:

"You have persevered in my trials with me. [They have shared in the penalties of lowly status.] I therefore assign to you a kingdom as my Father assigned to me, that in my kingdom you may feast at my table [where waiters become hosts] and sit on thrones ruling the twelve tribes of Israel [thrones where authority is exercised by slaves]" (22:28–30; cf. Rev. 3:20f.).

Just as he had presented himself in their midst as the most menial servant, so they would later channel into the apostolic community the authority they had received from this Father and this Son, through their continuance of his trials and self-humiliation. Luke discerned in Jesus' reference to their twelve thrones the antithesis to the thrones of the Gentile kings (22:25). According to the logic of the antithesis, just as God's assignment of the kingdom to Jesus had been vindicated by Jesus' "trials" in his role as a servant, so, too, Jesus' sharing of his authority with the apostles would be vindicated by their sharing his mission as servant. Wherever the act of serving would be repeated, there the authority of his kingdom would become operative. There, too, men would be seated both at the banquet table in the kingdom and at the meal in the Upper Room (22:27). As Principle B had released the healing and the saving power of God through the word and work of Jesus, so the same release would take place through the word and work of the apostles and, by implication, through the life of a community whose pattern of organization was determined by that authority. Wherever this authority was operative, the reality of meekness would simultaneously conceal and disclose the power of this God and this Messiah.

It is probable that Luke discerned in Peter's denial on that same evening an illustration of how Jesus' prophecy would be fulfilled. The prediction of his denial (22:34) implied Jesus' awareness that Peter had not yet grasped the power of Principle B or the degree to which Jesus' arrest and execution would demonstrate that power. This may explain why in spite of his desire to eat the Passover with Peter, Jesus would not do so until after Satan's trial of him (22:15–18). This trial proved not only the stubborn control of Peter's mind by Principle A but also the way in which Peter came to share in the trials of Jesus. The humiliation and subsequent repentance of Peter had, however, vindicated the power of Principle B and the subsequent ability of Peter to strengthen the church when it should undergo the same trials.

Luke discerned in this struggle over Peter's soul a picture of the continuing struggle between God and Satan. To him the "trials" of Jesus and Peter revealed nothing less than a decisive contest between two rulers for the salvation of the world. God was determined to end man's captivity to Satan, a captivity which could be terminated only when men were no longer blinded by the illusions of power. Such a recovery of sight had begun with the "today" of Jesus' proclamation (Lk. 4:18—21) and would continue with the Pentecostal witness (Acts 2:37—47). Implicit in the Gospel was the announcement of the transfer of power from one epoch to another. Men could shift from one kingdom to another by accepting the authority of the servant-king, by obeying his unconditional order and his unambiguous example, by adopting the stance of the younger, the weaker, the waiter. In his kingdom the hierarchy of power and the hierarchy of humility had fused into one. The place of fusion was the cross which had revealed to faith both the power of darkness (22:53) and the entering of Christ into his kingdom and glory (23:42; 24:26).

This type of thinking about the operation of authority forced Luke to rely upon parabolic rather than legalistic description. Parables enabled him to interpret the situation of the prophet-apostles in terms of their position as servants and masters simultaneously, responsible to their servant-master for exercising authority according to Principle B. Such an example is provided by the two parables in Luke 12:35—46. The first parable (vv. 35—37) pictured the disciples (12:22) as servants who were waiting for their master to come home from the marriage feast. What would happen should they be ready to welcome his knocking at the door? Contrary to all social custom but wholly in line with Jesus' behavior at the Last Supper, he would put on his apron, have them sit at table, and he would come to serve them. His lordship over them would be exercised by this act of humility—if they were ready.

This first parable, however, left undefined two things: what duties would they have as servants? In what ways would they display their readiness for his return? Both definitions were provided by a second parable (12:42–44). Their duties had been established by their role as his stewards, that is, they must provide food at regular and proper times for members of his household. Set over the others, they must place themselves under the others. It was by such self-humbling that they would prepare for his knocking, and become worthy to be served and to be given yet greater authority by him (44). Any neglect of this principle (that is, any use of their position to claim service *from* others) would produce total and immediate expulsion from his fellowship. Although these parables dramatize a modest domestic scene (the intimate obligations of a single household), Principle B was obviously meant to apply to all types of human associations, whether political or economic or religious. It constituted nothing less than the most revolutionary form of liberation from every kind of servitude, especially after the parabolic teaching of this prophet had been driven home by his parabolic action, namely, his crucifixion.

Luke's conception of Jesus' relation to his apostles is also reflected, though not so explicitly or certainly, in his use of the parable of field work and house work (17:7–10).[12] He visualized Jesus as the master and each apostle (17:5) as slave, inasmuch as this correlation of master/slave often appears in the Lucan parables (12:35–48; 14:15–24; 19:11–27; 20:9–17). The early Christian lexicon often compared the work of apostles to shepherding (Lk. 12:32; Acts 20:28; Mk. 6:34; I Cor. 9:7; Jn. 21:16; I Pt. 5:2f.) and plowing (I Cor. 3:6–9; 9:10; Lk. 9:62). Even more frequent was the image of them serving as deacons in preparing supper and waiting on tables. According to this parable, apostles were glad to do field work (shepherds) but wanted to avoid table service (deacons). This was precisely the situation described in Acts 6:1–6, when the twelve apostles arranged the appointment of seven deacons to do the less popular task, in spite of the recognition in Acts 1:25 that apostleship (*apostolē*) and service (*diakonia*) belonged to every apostle. It is also a situation reflected in

I Corinthians 9 where we learn of a conflict between Paul and other apostles over whether they should exploit their right to be fed by the congregations which they had established. In a Gospel where Jesus had permanently associated table service with messianic suffering (Lk. 22:14–22) and where he had taught that apostles would be judged in terms of their faithfulness to that type of service (12:35–46), this parable in its conclusion articulates the proper attitude of both master and slave:

> "Is [the master] grateful to the servant for carrying out his orders? So with you: when you have carried out all your orders, you should say, 'We are servants and deserve no credit; we have only done our duty' " (17:9–10 NEB).

Luke appealed to the notion of authority in many other passages; in them all we discern a radical rethinking of the way in which divine authority operates—from the bottom up. He saw all authority as derived from God, the Lord of heaven and earth (10:21). It is therefore within God's power to withhold from them the "times and seasons" which he has determined (Acts 1:7), for he alone has jurisdiction over both death and final destiny. This is what excludes all fear of any enemies and what should maximize a disciple's fear of God (12:4–5). Knowledge of God is available, but only under strict limitations; otherwise God remains hidden from the eyes of men (10:21–24), who naturally look for God in situations where Principle A rather than Principle B is operative. Only because Jesus had received authority from God did his word carry authority (4:32), whether to command unclean spirits (4:36) or to forgive sins (5:36). Jesus alone could reveal the Father, since only to him had the Father delivered all things (10:22). As we have seen, it was this same authority over "all the power of the enemy" which Jesus had granted first to the Twelve and then to the seventy-two. He remained the sole source of their authority, as God remained the source of his. But the functions of authority were identical: healing and teaching, blessing and cursing (10:16).

From the highest level to the lowest, the channeling of God's authority (*exousia*) came into conflict with an alternate power structure. The conflict developed in earnest after Jesus' rejection of the authority which Satan had offered him (4:6–13). At the end of Jesus' mission the conflict engaged the authority of Pilate (20:20) and Herod (23:7), along with all those gathered in Gethsemane for Jesus' arrest, when he declared "this is your hour and the power of darkness" (22:53). With the appearance of such a prophet, the question became inescapable: does he receive his authority from heaven or from men? With every successive expulsion of a demon, every cure of sickness, every act of forgiveness, that question became more urgent. Are such actions the result of Satan's power or of God's? Such a question could be answered rightly only by knowledge of the line of authority within which each stood.

So much by way of exposition of Luke's understanding of authority. It may not be convincing at every point to a modern analyst, but it should be intelligible as a coherent mode of describing the human situation. It conveys the truth that every person stands within a web of human relationships in which he both exercises authority over certain persons and stands under the authority of others. Moreover, we have all experienced many different types of authority, with conflicts emerging as they command contradictory actions. We know the types of command which come from those in higher echelons, as well as the types of pressures from those in lower. We are aware that by its nature authority is hidden; any effort to trace it to its source falls short of reaching the ultimate grounding. We know that some of the strongest incentives to action come from very mysterious places, from subterranean channels of social and personal existence. We know that any society weaves together many separate chains of authority, linking individuals and their various groups into patterns of obedience obligatory on all. I need not give a full analysis of the role of authority in Consciousness A. I want simply to suggest that this role, by analogy, can make intelligible many features of Consciousness B. Each of the eight structural girders in Luke's pattern of thinking permits an approach from this angle. For instance, if the present power of God is an opaque idea, it may become less opaque when we realize that wherever a man or a group yields to any authority as ultimate, there a particular deity stands revealed. So, too, the image of the kingdom, whether of God or of Satan, connotes in part that structure of forces which operates within a single synchronized hierarchy of authorities which determines the corporate behavior of competing groups. We must forego that exploration, however, and add here only a few notes to this chapter.

1. The relation between authority and rights. It is symptomatic that men today assume that these are mutually exclusive concepts, that is, I have a right to do something only when I have been freed *from* an overarching authority. The men of the New Testament had the almost opposite assumption, a sign of this fact being the use of the same word, *exousia,* to indicate both referents. As one definition of this Greek word, Bauer-Gingrich-Funk gives "freedom of choice, right to act, decide or dispose of one's property as one wishes." Another definition, apparently quite different, is this: "the power exercised by rulers or others in high position by virtue of their office." We have, I trust, seen how these two definitions are not incompatible but actually complementary. To be given authority over a specified arena, whether human or nonhuman, is to have a right to act with freedom within that arena. We receive liberty to do something when we have received authority over a particular arena of action. Each master is given rights over his own servant, all the while his own master exercises rights over him. When looking down the ladder, one can speak of rights; when looking up, one must speak of the obligation to obey.

2. The relation between authority and capacity. The conferring of authority also makes us competent and capable of doing whatever work is envisaged (a second definition in Bauer-Gingrich-Funk). The higher the authority the greater the capability that is conveyed to its recipient to accomplish the tasks assigned. To be under another's authority is to recognize his competence to command; to be set over another is to be granted a similar capacity and competence. To the extent that the direction of authority is reversed in

Consciousness B, to that same extent the notions of rights, freedom, and capacities will be transformed. If Satan and God are recognized as being at war, each trying to secure human obeisance to his authority, that warfare will focus upon the mutually exclusive systems of duties, freedoms, and capacities to which competing social or political movements appeal in their efforts to enlist supporters.

3. The relation between Luke and other New Testament authors. A study of three passages in other New Testament writings indicates a basic congruence with the Lucan pattern of thinking about the source, direction and operation of God's authority. Consider the Johannine image of Jesus as the shepherd and the contrast with other types of authority in John 10:7–18. The thief or the hireling thinks first of his own interest; the good shepherd thinks of the needs of his sheep. In fact, the good shepherd dies for the sheep, thus expressing his knowledge of the Father and the Father's knowledge of him. The power, right, or authority (*exousia*), which Jesus exercised in sacrificing himself for them had been granted to him by his Father, whose love had been channeled through the Son's love. Various terms are used to describe the resulting unity between God and Christ and the sheep; they are bound together by sharing the same gifts of knowledge, authority, freedom, love, and self-sacrifice. Though the vocabulary varies from Luke's account of the dialogue at the Last Supper, the reality is much the same.

Or consider Paul's treatment of apostolic authority in his struggle with antagonists in the church at Corinth (I Cor. 9:3–12). On the surface the issue seems different, yet beneath the surface the kinship can be detected. As an apostle set over his church, Paul asserted certain rights and a certain authority (*exousia*). His appointment had given him the right to expect financial support as well as other privileges. Yet Paul had become aware that the gospel effectively defined his authority in other terms, so that to exercise authority in his own interest would necessarily hinder the movement of the gospel (v. 12). His authority to preach that gospel had carried with it the obligation to make it free of charge. Though it had made Paul free of all men, that same authority had made him effectively and permanently the slave of all (v. 19). Luke's theology may have been different from Paul's in certain points, but in this respect they agreed: Paul thought of himself as a slave of all, a status which he tried to dramatize by his refusal to claim his apostolic rights. He has proved ever since to be a stubborn foe of Christians who have sought to increase their own power and rights by applying the logic of Principle A. Paul's attitude is well summarized by G. P. Wiles: "He understood this God-appointed and God-maintained authority to be most truly expressed in the lowliness and loving self-giving that had been demonstrated in the obedience of Jesus Christ."[13]

Finally, consider how the prophet John in the Apocalypse described that alternate power structure which had formed the kingdom of the beast (13:1–13). Satan, the dragon, the sea beast, and the men who worship them are bound together in a conspiracy to maintain the same throne and authority. When they challenge God and his saints they appear to succeed in establishing jurisdiction over every type of human society (v.7). But that realm is the realm of captivity and violence, totally separate from the realm inhabited by the slain Lamb and all the saints who prove faithful to him. The two realms are constituted by the two kinds of sovereignty effective within them. Wherever one pattern operates there is the Satanic kingdom; wherever the other, God's. A central clue to the boundary between them is the character of the authority being exercised.[14]

There is actually little that is novel in this exegesis of the Lucan passages. Every exegete has interpreted these texts in a fashion quite similar. Every preacher has a barrel of sermons on Christ the servant, who demanded that his followers become servants of men for God's sake. Every moralist has dealt with the implications of the parables and of the example of Jesus for shaping private spirituality and corporate piety. It is a novel experiment, however, to extend the range of relevance beyond that of individual morality or ecclesiastical ethos to encompass all power struggles that emerge in the realms of politics, international affairs, and industrial relations, and, beyond those realms, into the cosmological and ontological spheres. It is a novel experiment to use these texts as clues to the most intimate psychological conflicts and at the same time to discern the nexus between these and the most ultimate and universal conflicts that occur in heaven and on earth. Or that, at least, was Luke's conviction. The authority of Jesus as exemplified in the cross provides an ultimate resolution of all the conflicts in which persons and peoples engage.

A final question: is this conception of God's authority as mediated through Jesus intrinsically unintelligible? I do not think so. It may be foolish, but it is not unintelligible. What makes men unable to make sense of it is not its inherent unintelligibility but its unacceptability. It undermines the power of Consciousness A, and it has always done so. Such a threat to the dominant system of authorities can be repelled in various ways. It can always be branded as patent and blatant folly. Or its relevance can be limited to some restricted sectors of human existence, for example, to life within the Christian community. In any case, its claim to cosmological and ontological ultimacy must be rejected. Such a rejection proves relatively simple in an age where God is dead or so distant from the human scene as to be inactive in it, where the church has become the guardian of established mores and the mirror of conventional world views. It was not so simple in first-century Israel, where the aliveness of God was not in question and where men assumed his power to determine all destinies. In that situation the claim that God's authority had been fully disclosed in Christ's self-emptying (*kenosis*) became the rallying cry of a revolutionary counterculture which threatened every established institution. In that setting the structures of authority in Consciousness B were altogether too intelligible to be tolerated, except by those whose views of the world had been transformed by this silent revolution.

2

The role of an induna *in Rhodesia:*
The hands that held the kingdom had to be firm.
The shoulders on which the kingdom rested had to be
steady and strong. The eyes that saw for the kingdom
had to see far and near. They had to be more power-
ful than those of the ordinary man. The ears that
had to hear everything in the interest of the security
of the kingdom had to listen constantly. . . . He
could not live for himself. He lived first and foremost
for the kingdom. . . . He was in the kingdom and
the kingdom was in him. . . . He lost himself in
the kingdom, and those under his jurisdiction lost
themselves in him since to them he was that kingdom
in its visible and tangible form. [1]

THE SYMBOLISM OF HEAVEN

WE NOW TAKE UP the second stage in our effort to come to grips with that world view of Luke which we have called Consciousness B. We have focused attention on chapter 10 of the Gospel in order to establish a control over our more generalized reflections. That text has suggested a series of inferences concerning the operation of authority, the authority of Jesus and of his delegates, sufficiently akin to the structure of authority in any society to provide a basis for understanding and sufficiently central to any world view to illuminate other, less transparent attitudes. Among the least transparent to us is Luke's frequent and determinative references to a realm he called heaven. To him heaven was the originating source of all the various authorities operative in God's creation; it was the realm where such alternative invisible authorities as God and Satan were struggling for primacy. Let us examine this mode of thinking to see whether it is coherent and viable.

HEAVEN AS ANALOGY

I think that I need not cite extensive data to support the observation that heaven as a category of thought is foreign to Consciousness A. Scholars may not agree with all the various conclusions of Rudolf Bultmann, but there are few who contest his judgment that all references to heaven in Scripture utilize "the language of mythology" in which "we can no longer believe."[2] Even those who formally insist on their belief in heaven (as in the phrase in the Creed "he ascended into heaven") often betray an embarrassment in doing so, because such language is not really native to their daily vocabulary; the realm called heaven does not really form the conscious context of their living. Bultmann's scepticism is virtually coextensive with the modern western mentality, in which men assume that heaven is part of a primitive cosmology, an archaic picture of the universe as a three-story house: heaven, earth, hell. Since that picture is obsolete, the term itself has virtually disappeared except for use by poets or other eccentrics. It is by no means certain, however, that Luke shared so primitive a cosmology. With other New Testament writers, he had accepted conventional ways of using cosmological metaphors to point to ontological realities. Although the metaphor was spatial, the reality was not. The Greek word *ouranos* covered a vast range of meanings which cannot be telescoped into a single limited referent, for example, the top floor of man's living space. Of course biblical writers referred, on occasion, to the visible canopy of the sky ("The sky is red, so weather should be fair tomorrow" [Mt. 16:2]); but usually the context indicates a freer play of the imagination. When we insist on a literalistic reading of their thought, we may miss entirely what they were trying to convey. In treating them as literalists we may prove ourselves more naive and even more literalist than they.

A parable used by Karl Barth in 1920 may clarify the point. He describes a man standing inside his house looking out through the window at passersby. As he watches, these people start looking up into the sky, shading their eyes, craning their necks, intent on something which, because of the low ceiling of his living room, lies outside his own range of vision. Like those passersby, biblical authors are keenly aware of a world far beyond the usual span of our ordinary attention. Because they are not limited by man-made ceilings, their range of vision is correspondingly greater. To see what they see, we need to leave our living space and move into theirs.[3] Although Barth's analogy is very suggestive, it has obvious limitations. Biblical writers did not try to penetrate God's purposes by staring up into the sky, nor did they call on their readers to do so. They could utilize the analogical suggestiveness of the sky without becoming stargazers.

To trace the figurative use of heaven in the Old Testament, a tradition of which Luke was heir, would fill a large volume. The height of the sky above the earth suggested the transcendence of God, its omnipresence suggested his nearness. The heavens combine elements of invisibility and visibility, hiddenness and disclosure. They display the glory, the majesty, and the mystery of God, the light which men see and the light by which they see. They remind men of the multiple connotations of day and night, darkness and light. Many analogies were discovered between the movements of sun, moon, and stars and the historical experiences of Israel. Here is the source of rain and snow, the stage across which clouds scud, thunders roll, and lightnings flash, all eliciting reflections concerning God's ways with men. His throne is in the heavens, and from that vantage point he can see everything which happens within the hearts of men (Ps. 33:13–15). No literature makes more of the figural richness of the sky than does the Bible. If a comparison should be made between biblical and modern capacities for profiting from that wealth, it is the modern mind that is poverty-stricken. The dominance of the alleged scientific mentality with regard to the heavens has seriously diminished the imaginative faculties of men and women.[4]

The contrast between Consciousness A and Consciousness B, however, is much more than a matter of dexterity in the use of analogies. Where heaven is taken most seriously it connotes the basic and abiding context for man's existence, a context even more vivid and complex than that of earth. The community has its origin and destiny in heaven; its vocation comes thence and its accounts must be rendered there; it lives "before" and "in the sight of" heaven. Especially is this true of the prophet who is sent from heaven where he has stood in the counsels of God, having heard and seen things otherwise invisible and inaudible. To him a door has been opened into heaven. Whether mediated in dreams, through angels, or by the Holy Spirit, God's word has emanated from this realm as directly as by a trumpet blast. The prophet's work is punctuated by his dialogue with heaven; the fire burns in his bones until he can complete each assignment. Such an assignment would have been futile apart from an audience to whom heaven was just as real and just as decisive as to him, an audience which recognized its need for the prophet's eyes and ears and which could be addressed as "citizens of heaven," aware that at no point could its earthly existence be sundered from this invisible environment. There was nothing dubious about this reality. This realm was as substantial, as densely populated, as inescapable, as any feature of human experience. When we recall how essential and complex this category was in biblical thinking, the very effort to rehabilitate it becomes presumptuous and ridiculous. And yet it is even more absurd that modern Christians have so estranged themselves from Consciousness B as to require such an effort, all the while they boast of being mature enough to know that heaven does not exist.

Let me mention two signs of this estrangement. The first is the tendency that prompts modern men to equate heaven with another world, and to assume that to use such a category spells an obsolete form of otherworldliness. This is quite mistaken. As H. Traub shows, the biblical accent upon the transcendence of God does not imply his separation from history or from the earth; heaven is the place of perpetual nearness to God.[5] And as Amos Wilder has argued, heaven was understood to be the place where antagonistic powers were engaged in battle for human allegiance: "Believers were shaping a new pattern of the human community and realizing very concrete social values in a widening movement which collided increasingly with existing institutions and vested interests, economic, social and political."[6]

A second sign is to be seen in the widespread acceptance of Rudolf Bultmann's program for demythologizing the message of the New Testament. If we refuse to accept the "mythological" character of heaven, as New Testament thinkers construed it, the whole program is altered. Such a program would not have become so popular had heaven remained a meaningful and viable category of thought. In other words, it was only because the mind of modern western man had first been de-propheticized that it became conscious of the need for demythologizing. Our mentality had already lost its ability to comprehend the reality of heaven as the necessary ground of the prophet's experience and authority. Since this is true, it is not enough for theologians to refute Bultmann's concept of myth. Such a refutation is pointless until there is a renewed capacity to apprehend the reality to which the term heaven points.

HEAVEN AND THE PROPHET'S AUTHORITY

Enough now of such generalizations. We must turn back to examine specific texts in Luke's account of the commissioning of the seventy-two evangelists. When they returned from their first excursion they were enthusiastic. "Even the demons," they said, "obeyed us when we used your name" (i.e., when we appealed to your authority). Jesus' reply seems to be a nonsequitur, for it is couched in quite different terms. "I have been watching Satan fall like lightning from heaven. . . . I have given you authority" (10:18–19). His statement must in some way have been linked to theirs. Can we reduce that link to an algebraic equation: $a:b::a^1:b^1$?

his authority : their authority :: Satan's fall from heaven : the demons' obedience

To Jesus came the prophetic vision of an event in heaven; his missionaries saw the consequences of that event in the cities of Israel. Virtually the same equation is this:

Satan : Jesus :: the demons : the seventy-two

What had happened had been the freeing of certain men from demons. But that happening had disclosed not two but four active participants. The field of force was a parallelogram, for it was viewed as the battleground between God and Satan, and, simultaneously, between these messengers and the demons.

There are, of course, many dangers in reducing personal relations to algebraic equations of this sort. Nevertheless, such equations have their value in clarifying the cluster of convictions implied in the dialogue.

In the liberation of certain men, God was reaping his harvest; Jesus was in a position to tell his messengers how their new powers had become accessible through the expulsion of Satan from heaven. These new powers had been both disclosed and hidden by their healing work; it required the word of a prophet to lay bare the origin and character of those powers. Jesus stood at the junction of the two worlds, saying, "I was watching. . . . I have given you. . . ." At that junction his special knowledge and his power were essential to their mission. Heaven served as the essential source of that knowledge and power. This text clarifies one feature of prophetic revelation: because an invisible reality had been operative behind and within a visible event, the prophet was called on to make clear the significance of that sign. The act of exorcism was the sign; the prophet disclosed its significance. Undoubtedly Luke saw this episode as a phase of the training by which Jesus' messengers could become prophets (revealers of heavenly truth) and kings (mediators of heavenly power) in their own right (10:23–24; Acts 3:1–16). The episode implies that the effective transmission of heavenly power was an essential element in the prophet's work. It is therefore a clue which we dare not neglect if we hope to understand his consciousness. For him there existed a direct correlation between heaven and power: that power was defined by its heavenly origin, and heaven was defined by that power. In other words, to locate heaven one should trace that power to its source.

This correlation is clearly presupposed in another story: Luke 20:1–8, probably borrowed by Luke from Mark 11:27–33. The place was the temple in Jerusalem. The time was Passion Week and the climax of the struggle between Jesus and the leaders of Israel. The occasion was a question posed by those leaders: "By what authority do you do these things?" At stake was the loyalty and support of God's covenant community, together with the redemption of that community. The episode is rich in implications which can be drawn with a high degree of confidence. The formulation of the question implies that the issue of authority was recognized as more central than the issue of what Jesus had been doing—presumably his daily teaching (19:47), his dramatic entry into the city and the cleansing of the temple (19:28–45), his cures, exorcisms, and parables. These actions were not under debate; what was being contested was the authority for doing them. Jesus' counter-question focused upon two possibilities: the authority derived either from heaven or from men; but he left the choice open. (This episode seems to leave out of the reckoning a third option, adopted elsewhere by these same adversaries, that is, that the authority came from Beelzebub.) It is clear that both sides accepted Jesus' formulation of the question. Moreover, both assumed that the answer with respect to John the Baptist would apply to Jesus as well. If "from men" were the right answer, opposition to what Jesus had been doing would be called for, since any justification for his open challenge to the temple, the city, and the establishment would no longer exist. If "from heaven" were the right answer, his work would call for immediate and unconditional acceptance on the part of God's people. By replying to their question with another question, Jesus put them on the defensive: their answer would carry with it their decision. They avoided the trap by confessing their inability or their unwillingness to reach a decision. Jesus, in turn, refused to answer their question.

Jesus' refusal in this instance is in striking contrast to the disclosure of his authority when he commissioned the seventy-two messengers. In that case his word about heaven had corresponded to their obedience and their success in exorcisms. In this case his refusal to disclose heavenly truth corresponded to Pharisaic evasiveness, to their blindness to the truth. In both cases the objective reality was conjoined to the subjective response. Heaven as the source of Jesus' authority (the objective referent) actually became inseparable from human knowledge, decision, and action (the subjective referent). The prophet's vision of the invisible confronted his audience with an acceptance or rejection of his word as a decisive basis for action. Thus the work of the prophet became a polarizing agent, inasmuch as the response to that work created two communities increasingly at odds with each other. The question "from heaven or from men?" speeded up the processes by which these two communities became disjoined. Although these processes derived from the initiative of heaven, their earthly reality was not thereby diminished. Many scholars trace Jesus' final condemnation by religious and governmental leaders to his challenge in the temple cleansing. Etienne Trocmè, for instance, gives a persuasive sketch of this interpretation.[7]

Can equations be devised which convey this analysis of Luke's story, in which Jesus' authority is correlated to that of John? I believe that the following four equations are justified:

> authority from heaven : unlimited obedience :: authority from man : refusal of obedience
>
> John's authority : Jesus' authority :: those baptized by John : those following Jesus
>
> John's authority : Jesus' authority :: those rejecting John : those rejecting Jesus
>
> authority from heaven : one community :: rejection of that authority : a hostile community

In calling attention to these correspondences we have been applying rules which have been employed since the earliest stages of biblical criticism. Where two texts present ideas that parallel each other,
each can be used to throw light on the other. In this case, the interpreter should begin with the more transparent idea and then
move to the more obscure.[8] So we have been interpreting Luke 10 by
Luke 20; in both chapters heavenly origins were seen to parallel
earthly actions. In both chapters the origins, being hidden, required
a prophetic vision and this vision in turn polarized two hostile communities. Behind this type of thinking, a correlation is assumed to
exist between heaven and the invisible that may be expressed thus:

heaven : the invisible :: earth : the visible

In this respect Barth is entirely justified in identifying heaven with
"the sum of all that which in creation is unfathomable, distant, alien
and mysterious."[9] But because the crucial issue is the character of
competing authorities, this equation must be accompanied by
another:

heaven : one source of authority :: earth : a competing source

And because the two authorities correspond to two communities,
this equation must be associated with another:

heaven : one community :: earth : a hostile community

By these equations we seek to take account of patterns of thinking
reflected in the text of Luke 20. Although there is a correlation between heaven and hiddenness, the hiddenness is not the same for all
participants, since what is seen by some is not seen by others. This
variation is produced by differences in man's readiness to hear and to
obey the prophet's word. In chapter 20 the hiddenness is a factor in a
total situation characterized by the "ignorance" of the adversaries
and by the prophet's refusal to answer their question.

In chapter 10 the differences between the two audiences receive a
somewhat different articulation:

In that same hour he [Jesus] rejoiced in the Holy Spirit and said, "I thank thee, Father, Lord of heaven and earth, that thou hast hidden these things . . . and revealed them . . . " (v.21).

The grammatical structure suggests several inferences. God's lordship over heaven and earth appears to include power over both the visible and the invisible; this means that he has power both to hide and to disclose.

the invisible : the visible :: God's action in hiding : his action in disclosing

This double action with regard to the same "things" is presumably a phase of his governance as creator and as ruler of heaven and earth. So, because the boundary between heaven and earth follows the horizon of the visible, that boundary varies according to the creator's decision to hide or to reveal. Moreover, this decision represents something more than divine impulsiveness or the realm of chance and accident in history. God's decision determines the identity, the status, and the destiny of the two very specific historical communities. In this respect, not seeing is to damnation as seeing is to salvation. Thus we can extend the chain of equations:

God's decision to hide : damnation :: God's decision to reveal : salvation

This equation gives full weight to the biblical perceptions of divine determinism. God's residence in heaven is related to his freedom to decide for or against men. "Our God is in the heavens; he does whatever he pleases" (Ps. 115:3).

HEAVEN AND MEN'S EYES

But this articulation of God's creative freedom does not exclude a corresponding freedom of decision on man's part.

God's hiding : blind eyes :: God's revealing : seeing eyes

Earlier we were inclined to correlate heavenly authority with the objective reality, the recognition of that authority with the subjective reality. The text now compels us to recognize that God is active within the subjective factor, within man's recognition of heavenly authority. Although God's action remains other than man's action, it is not thereby separated from man's vision; although man's vision remains his own action, it is not thereby separated from God's action. God creates both the light which is seen and the light by which men see. The same interdependence applies to heaven.

It is extremely important for Luke's readers to grasp this fusion of divine with human wills in the idea of heaven, for the fusion rules out the use of any quantitative formula for mapping the boundaries of heaven. It is not a place which can be located independently of God and men. The heaven of those who can see is not the same as the heaven of those who cannot; those differences are not to be measured by the medical doctor or by the astronomer. Because blindness or sight are correlated with a realm where divine and human wills intersect, they can be measured only by the prophet who has access simultaneously to the mysteries of God's will and those of the human heart. We ask, therefore, concerning further determinants of the human wills and human hearts corresponding, on the one hand, to the ability to see and, on the other, to God's decision to reveal his will through the prophet. To this query the Lucan text furnishes an important clue:

> "You have hidden these things from the wise and understanding and disclosed them to babes. . . . Blessed are the eyes which see what you see!" (10:21,23)

This fresh element in the construction may be shown by these equations:

God's revealing : the babes :: God's hiding : the wise
seeing eyes : the babes :: blind eyes : the wise

Implicit in this text is the recognition that this division into two communities (of wise and babes) has produced an astonishing reversal of human expectations. Men expect the wise to be able to see and to comprehend the invisible and the heavenly. But in this as in many other respects Luke exemplifies the thought of Isaiah's declaration: " 'My thoughts are not your thoughts,' says the Lord." In fact, Isaiah had seen in this contrast between God's ways and man's a major component of the distinction between heaven and earth (55:8–9). For both Isaiah and Luke the central concern is to understand God's surprising ways of dealing with his covenant community. The key terms *wise* and *babes* point to two hostile communities, separated by boundaries which have been disclosed by the mission of Jesus and the seventy-two, and by the journey toward Jerusalem which they share. The community of babes corresponds precisely to the community which recognizes and obeys that type of authority which we explored in the previous chapter. A song currently sung by the "Jesus people" to guitar accompaniment is not far from the mark: "You gotta be a baby to go to heaven."

This whole analysis of the conflict between the babes and the wise appears highly theoretical until one recalls the fact that throughout his two volumes Luke identifies the babes with the powerless poor and the wise with the powerful rich (of which we shall say more in the next chapter). So when these two groups are described as blind or as able to see, the boundary between them is seen to follow the line between those who adopt Jesus' criteria of power and those who reject those criteria. Should they reject those criteria, poor people become as blind as the rich. The operative question is not economic status but the definition of power. Hence the following equation:

blind eyes : one idea of power :: seeing eyes : an alternative idea

If now we collate the series of images which Luke associated with heaven, we note some intriguing parallels:

the community of babes
the seeing eyes
the poor

those who accept Jesus' definition of power
the source of the prophet's authority
God's action in revealing
the healing of blindness
invisible things

Consciousness B is structured by the interdependence of these terms.
But it is very significant that these terms no longer represent particular spaces; rather they point to the complex spiritual interdependence of persons and communities—the Father, the Son, the
prophets, the babes, the wise. Luke's use of language, including
vocabulary, syntax, and images, is a way of explicating that interdependence as well as the antagonisms that constitute those two
communities. These modes of thought derive from basic vocations in
the world. The functions of such terms as *heaven* and *earth* are integral to that way of living and speaking. References to such environ-
mental images serve to express the distance between the wise and the
babes, a contrast which corresponds to the distance between God's
election or rejection, his revelation or hiddenness.

In Luke 10:23–24 still another contrast is indicated: "Many
prophets and kings desired to see what you see and did not see it."
This raises the question of the connection between the babes and the
missionaries; it suggests a new equation:

missionaries : babes :: prophets and kings : Israel

Just as babes have been chosen to receive the disclosure (v. 21), so,
too, these missionaries have been appointed as revealers and rulers,
the successors to prophets and kings. The appointment has been
sealed by what they see and hear, that is, a disclosure of truth and a
delegation of authority. This appointment is not presented as a
put-down of earlier prophets and kings, but as a recognition and
completion of their work. It would seem that Luke saw heaven as the
source of that knowledge and authority which had been mediated by
the entire chain of spokesmen who had disclosed God's covenant

with Israel, the community of babes, from the beginning. The history of what had happened in heaven is the other side of the history of this earthly community, revealed, through its leaders, to babes but hidden from the wise.

Still another aspect of this history is implied in Luke 10:22. Although many "things" had been delivered to the Son, one "thing" is decisive—the Son's ability to reveal who the Father is.

> "No one knows who the Son is except the Father, or who the Father is except the Son and anyone to whom the Son chooses to reveal him."

Here the distinction between heaven and earth appears as a corollary to the distinction between knowledge of the Father and ignorance of him. Heaven is a realm that subsists under the authority of Father, Son, and Spirit, who together reveal their presence to "babes." Knowledge of this presence is assumed to be of primary importance. To know this Father is to dwell in this heaven; conversely, this means that the problem of heaven is identical with the problem of God. Here a correlation appears between pride in one's own wisdom and unawareness of God, both expressed in this context as failure to comprehend the invisible reality of heaven. This saying assumes that the Son and the Father are really invisible, but also that they are invisibly real.[10] These are, as Barth has shown, complementary aspects of heaven. The character of this invisible reality is clarified by this specific text, which traces the recognition of the Son to God's "gracious will" and the recognition of the Father to the Son's choice. With other early Christians Luke realized both the invisibility and the reality of such a will and such a choice. To see and to hear such a disclosure seem to have been the essential credentials of the prophet-king as well as the internal substance of the knowledge conferred on the babes.

Since the Son was disclosed as the slave whose authority operated through his humiliation, knowledge of the Father could be disclosed only to babes in their lowliness and only to prophets in their obedient sharing in their master's humiliation. This is an important point to which we will return, but it must not be obscured by other links in this chain of ideas. Here we glimpse Luke's understanding of the chief steps by which men receive access to heavenly matters: from the Father to the Son to the contemporary successors of prophets and kings, to the poor who reconstitute Israel. Moreover, each step is characterized by that movement of authority (of kingship) which we have called Principle B.

Still another text suggests further nuances concerning the relation of these prophet-kings to heaven. According to Jesus their joy should flow from the fact that their names have been inscribed in heaven (Lk. 10:20). What frame of reference makes cogent this correlation of joy with names in heaven? Profound mysteries lurk here which can be comprehended only by the sharpest of sensitivities. Something had happened to these men which should be more productive of joy than even the gift of power over demons; this happening had changed their names, that is, the innermost structure of their selfhood. Apparently they had received adoption into a new family. The inscription of names signifies a new vocation within that family; in being called from heaven and sent from heaven they were given a new beginning and a new ending. We are surely not far wrong in asserting that in Luke's mind what had happened to them had changed the orientation of their existence, transforming the core of selfhood (their names), together with its outermost environment (heaven). This notion says something important about heaven: it is the "place" where these men now live, it is the "place" of utter rejoicing, where they receive by means of the Spirit new knowledge of the Father and of the Son. Again we observe the link between hiddenness and *kenosis*. Again it becomes obvious that this knowledge of heaven conveyed to them a clear and compelling sense of their own identity as babes and their vocation as prophets.[11]

HEAVEN AND THE SPIRIT

The implicit correlation between heaven, sonship, and calling as a prophet becomes explicit in the account of Jesus' baptism (3:21–

22), when it was declared that Jesus' name as Son had been disclosed as the will of the Father in heaven. The opening of heaven had made visible and audible the inner meaning of this event; this disclosure had conveyed the fact of Jesus' sonship and of God's fatherhood, both as expressions of God's gracious will. The agent of disclosure had been the Holy Spirit; the recipient, a penitent man in the midst of a penitent Israel—the implication being that this baptism represented and included the baptism of all believers. In his baptism each penitent received the seal of his own sonship by way of the same Spirit. In this context heaven was viewed as the distinctive source and context of new life as God's sons and as heirs of the kingdom. This became the realm of new creation, whence emerged the new world of the new humanity, united in a new vocation.

This perspective makes intelligible two features in Luke's understanding of the Christian's prayer. We call attention first to a petition which may well have originally stood in the Lucan text of the Lord's Prayer: "Let thy Holy Spirit come upon us and cleanse us."[12] Second, we note Luke's assurance that *from heaven* the Father will give the Holy Spirit to all his children who ask him (11:13). Heaven is assumed to be the source of the Holy Spirit and of all the gifts of that Spirit to the church. Luke saw the boundary between heaven and the life of the believer as entirely open to this free movement of the Spirit; the believer depended each day upon daily traffic between the two realms. Because a person's name is written *there,* its potencies enable his deeds of faith *here.* His treasures, along with his heart, belong *there* (12:33–34); his humiliation as God's son occurs *here.* Heaven thus becomes intelligible as the hidden source of sonship and of all the gifts of the Spirit which empower the earthly life of those sons. Since this is true, each successive manifestation of any such gift becomes a reminder of the actuality of heaven and of the citizenship of the believer.

Far from being spacebound or timebound, Luke's notion of heaven transcended space and time without thereby becoming spaceless or timeless. Geographical distances between Tyre, Sidon, Chorazin, Bethsaida, and Capernaum were bridged by the fact that all these cities would be accountable to the same judgment (10:13–15). The notion of heaven reflected the conviction that men everywhere are accountable before the same court. All spaces are comprehended as having the same horizon. So, too, the idea of heaven bridged the distances in time between Noah, Lot, and the seventy-two messengers (17:20–30). Where space and time might otherwise be assumed to separate men of different generations and countries, in Luke's thought heaven was able to unite them all under one canopy without erasing temporal distinctions. Just as in heavenly glory Jesus conversed on the mountain with Moses and Elijah, so, too, he assured his servants that they would attend a banquet with ancient patriarchs and prophets in his kingdom (13:28–29). In Peter's experience of transfiguration, Jesus was seen to be closer to Moses and Elijah than to the men who executed him.[13]

Just as past epochs were made contemporaneous by this accessibility of heaven, so, too, future epochs were also already manifest in heaven. It was because of the disclosure of heavenly secrets that prophets could proclaim God's promises as the ground for future hopes and fears. All references to the future return of the Messiah or to the coming of his kingdom presupposed an advent *from heaven,* where Jesus was already enthroned and was therefore ruling his kingdom. Only because of this origin could the covenant community accept the promises of Jesus as conveying present power to his followers. Thus Consciousness B embodied the awareness of the contemporaneity of all epochs, whereas modern readers instinctively see those epochs as separate.

This feature of New Testament thought has almost totally baffled twentieth-century readers. We can make sense of the idea of the kingdom as a future utopia, more or less distant, or as a reality internalized within present spiritual experiences. But we meet in the New Testament writers like Luke who fuse future expectations with present experiences in their conceptions of the kingdom of God. It is this fusion which distinguishes Consciousness B from Consciousness A and which baffles modern readers. I believe that there is no intelligible resolution of this apparent contradiction so long as we try to peg the ideas about the kingdom of God to a fixed though imaginary time line of earthly history in which future and present simply cannot be compresent. A time line that is neatly divided into units of centuries provides little space for locating the plumb line of God's justice (Amos 7: 7–9) and even less space for indicating the power line of God's grace (Lk. 1: 68–79). But when we relate the idea of the kingdom to God's effective sovereignty and then try to grasp the multiple ways in which his sovereignty in heaven becomes manifest on earth, it becomes in fact necessary to account both for the future (but imminent) coming of the kingdom in fulfillment of God's promise and Israel's hope, and for the active incursion of that kingdom in gifts to his people of knowledge, obedience, and power. Within this consciousness it was entirely natural to speak of the names of the apostles as being written in heaven and of Satan falling from heaven, both events being grasped as present manifestations of things to come. As W. Pannenberg has well said, in the biblical way of thinking "events that are to be revealed in the end-time already pre-exist in heaven. . . . God is already ruling the world from the hiddenness of heaven. . . . The eschatological future is already present, although in secrecy and mystery which is the essence of heaven."[14] In the biblical consciousness heaven was the primary reality and the kingdom of God was the manifestation of that reality through the intervention of the Holy Spirit with his gifts of vocation and power. Heaven was frequently viewed as the place, incomparable to any other, "where God's planned salvation is already present prior to its working out on earth," the place where everything earthly is pre-existent, including, especially, the kingdom of God and of the Son of man.[15]

This accounts for the significance of heaven as the place of communication and communion where men can have traffic with God by way of prayer and worship. This function is suggested by a phrase in the story of Jesus feeding the five thousand in the wilderness, a story saturated with liturgical symbolism. After Jesus had taught and healed this crowd, and after the Twelve had seen the need for food but had confessed their own impotence to supply it, we find this sentence: "And taking the five loaves and the two fish, he *looked up to heaven* and blessed and broke them and gave them to the disciples to set before the crowd" (9:16). This reference to heaven seems quite unnecessary to us, but to the evangelists it was not. What did it signify to them? We might conjecture various intentions:

1. to show Jesus' total dependence on God
2. to give an illustration of his desire to seek God's will
3. as a conventional gesture in giving thanks
4. as a pattern to be followed in eucharistic services
5. to show that only heavenly food would suffice for this hunger
6. to call to mind the bond between this bread and the manna from heaven that had sustained Israel during the Exodus (Ex. 16:4)

We cannot be certain of Luke's conscious intention, but we believe that this is more than a thoughtless and perfunctory phrase. Heaven as the source of this bread, as the context for this "sign," makes intelligible a correlation among this feeding, the miraculous sustenance during the Exodus, the eucharistic meals of the church, and the banquet in the coming kingdom of God. Luke interpreted each meal with Jesus as carrying this range of potential meanings.

In this setting we may well recall the problem raised by the Greek adjective which is used to modify the noun *bread* in the Lord's Prayer. "Give us from day to day our *epiousion* bread" (Lk. 11:3). It is unlikely that "daily" is an accurate translation of *epiousion*. Translators make more or less intelligent guesses: supersubstantial bread, supernatural bread, our rations for tomorrow. I am inclined to think of this petition for bread as parallel to the petition for the kingdom. To receive this bread is to share each day in the heavenly banquet which enabled this army to continue its march. The bread comes from above, from heaven; to rely upon God's gift of strength from heaven is as necessary to this army as to lay up its treasures in heaven. Its daily meals embodied that fusion of heavenly gift and earthly vocation which permeated its life as a whole. Under Consciousness B men lived at the juncture of these two realms. The other petitions in the Lord's Prayer presuppose the same fusion: the action of God in forgiving men is conjoined to their own action; his delivering them from the Evil One coincided with their liberation from earthly trials.

Awareness of this fusion must become acute before prayer and worship can attain the imaginative depth which they had for Luke and his brothers. Until it does, the stories of the birth of Jesus will embarrass the contemporary church, for these stories belong in the habitat of worship where heaven connotes the realized presence of God in the full mystery of his glory.[16] For example, the nexus between heaven and earth is expressed in the cry of the army of angels:

"Glory to God in the highest [i.e., in heaven]
And on earth peace among men with whom he is pleased" (2:14).

This seems to imply a basic relationship:

heaven : God's glory :: earth : men's peace

The two realities seem to be interdependent in such a way that the more glory the more peace, and the more peace the more glory. The angels celebrate events in which this connection has become clear:

God's glory : men's peace :: heaven : earth

Such logic seems to be what underlies the fact that the messengers whose names were written in heaven (10:20) could shout "Shalom" to the homes which received them (10:5). So, too, the army of angels who appeared to the shepherds (an image of Christian leaders) easily eliminated the distance between heaven and earth when they proclaimed the "good news of a great joy" (2:10). The joy of the angels was simply the counterpart of the joy of men. The heavenly nimbus surrounds the shepherds watching their flocks by night. Like the seventy-two shepherds of chapter 10, they saw and heard things which prophets and kings had long hoped to see and hear;

because the message of the angels came from a realm that transcended time and space, it could convey glory and peace simultaneously to many groups at various times. For Luke to say "heaven" was to suggest the mysterious dimensions of that reality which had evoked such actual emotions as reverence, fear, joy, thanksgiving, wonder, whenever those emotions were prompted by the initiatives of divine grace among "men with whom he is pleased."

Luke envisaged the angels standing on the boundary between heaven and earth, engaged in a double activity: praising God and giving his message to men. He envisaged the work of the prophets similarly: they were expected to lead God's people in the same double activity. This is actually one way of understanding the Pentecost story in which Joel's prophecy was fulfilled. Here the Spirit enabled all believers to worship God (*glossolalia*) and to proclaim his peace to men who had come from all corners of the earth.

Luke visualized disciples as living within this dual environment; for example, sin is committed "before heaven" and repentance is the occasion for "joy in heaven" (15:7, 18, 21). I have argued elsewhere that the birth stories well represent the editorial perspectives of this evangelist.[17] I now contend that they reflect the mood and spirit which is characteristic of communal worship that expresses what I have called Consciousness B. I doubt if that consciousness, that perceptual vision of reality, will ever become fully intelligible apart from imaginative participation in Christian worship.

Heaven and Sonship

Perhaps this is the place to comment on a christological problem that continues to baffle exegetes. How can the New Testament be so inconsistent in its references to the point in time at which Jesus became God's Son? From the two volumes of this author, four different points in time could be selected, with evidence that each constituted the true beginning. In Acts, the day of begetting is at times identified with the day of resurrection and glorification (2:36; 3:13), an attitude made entirely explicit by the citation of Ps. 2:7 in Acts

13:33. In the Gospel, certain traditions seem to focus upon the manifestation of sonship to the apostles at the moment of the transfiguration (9:35; the saying of Jesus in 10:22 may refer back to this incident). Other traditions imply that his sonship was initiated at the baptism; the devil's "If you are the Son of God" (4:3, 9) and the textual variant of 3:22 ("today I have begotten thee") appear to substantiate this position. Finally, the birth narratives trace divine sonship to the moment of conception by the Holy Spirit (1:31, 35). To a modern reader this medley of answers to the same question bristles with contradictions, but there is no sign that Luke was troubled by them. He was not under compulsion to schedule such an event at a single spot on a single time line; he could readily accept the attitude of all four traditions. Why so? The answer must surely involve the whole complex of his attitudes toward heaven and its capacity to transcend earth's times.[18] God is not limited by the times of his appointment in the same ways as men are limited. Events which transpire at different times on man's calendar may spring from a single divine decision. To speak of Christ's sonship is a way of describing his heavenly vocation, not the sequences of an earthly diary. His sonship is a mystery of divine creation, adoption, and redemption; consequently only God can reveal to men who his Son is (10:22). Although no algebraic equation can do justice to such matters, this pattern of ideas might suggest this:

heaven : earth :: God's calling as son : the fulfillment of that calling

One stylistic characteristic of Luke should be noted here. On the occasion of each decisive revelation of God's will, he stressed some visible earthly component. At the ascension, the witnesses saw clouds and angels (Lk. 24:51; Acts 1:10); at the resurrection appearance Jesus ate a piece of broiled fish (Lk. 24:43); at the transfiguration he appeared in dazzling clothes (Lk. 9:29); at the baptism the Spirit descended in bodily form, as a dove (Lk. 3:22); and at conception and birth men saw a medley of various signs. This style of expression may well have been Luke's way of stressing the actuality of the strategic events, in part to counteract Gnosticizing tendencies in the church of his day. In our own reactions to his story we can all too readily misconstrue his rhetoric. We can confuse his account of the ascension (Acts 1:9–11) with the very clumsy and naive idea of space travel, a trip into the sky which would be matched by a later descent. The physical aspects of the ascent were, however, quite secondary to Luke's desire to underscore the actuality of the exaltation of Jesus to a position of greater authority and wider jurisdiction. As descent from heaven was implicit in the mission on which Jesus had been sent, so ascent into heaven was a way of affirming the completion of that mission (Jn. 7:33; 16:5). As his ascension marked the beginning of the mission of the disciples, so its completion would be marked by his return. Thus the vocabulary of heaven corresponded to the conditions and tenure of the disciples' vocation. This is why the apostles were rebuked for stargazing (Acts 1:11); the important thing was to get on with their work, as soon as the Holy Spirit should provide the requisite signs and gifts.[19]

That is what happened at Pentecost, when the Risen Lord, having received this gift from the Father, poured it out on them. They could now discern what had happened in heaven, as did the shepherds in Luke 2. The man whom Israel had crucified had been made both Lord and Christ (Acts 2:32–36). To accept that lordship was to accept the status and tasks of servants sent by him to the very people who had crucified him. To speak of his enthronement in heaven was to recognize his regal authority over earth. Only in his name or by his authority could men be saved (Acts 4:12). His heavenly exaltation carried as a corollary this intense particularism of promise and threat. But it also carried as another corollary an unlimited universalism, for he had been made both the Messiah of Israel and the ruler of the Gentiles. His heavenly power was disclosed in the boldness with which the apostles prayed and preached (Acts 4:27–31). The story of Stephen offered an effective profile of the relation between the heavenly Lord and his prophetic servants. Any onlooker could see Stephen standing before his tormentors; only Stephen could see the glory of God and Jesus standing before God's right hand. This vision vindicated his authority as a prophet and sealed his fate. The Holy Spirit enabled him to comprehend how his own stoning had become the point where the two realms met, in fulfillment of Jesus' own prophecy (Lk. 11:47–51). Similar paradigms may be found in the visions of heaven by Paul (Acts 9:3–6) and Peter (Acts 10:11–16). In every case the heavenly vision was the counterpart of an aspect of apostolic vocation. This relationship might be expressed thus:

apostolic vocation : human situation :: heavenly vision : normal vision

To that feature of the nexus between heaven and earth we will return in chapter 6.

This brings us back to the perceptive world of Luke 10, where Jesus' vision of heaven disclosed the heavenly counterpart to the earthly experience of his messengers. To Luke, three convictions appear to provide the rationale for his witness: the authority of Jesus and his messengers derived from the shared experience of self-denial and lowliness; this experience, this stance, served to hide the powerful presence of God; the vision of heaven served to disclose to "babes" what was hidden and so to confirm the authority by which they proclaimed good news to Israel. If we can grasp the correlation in Consciousness B between the concepts of authority and heaven we will immediately perceive the importance of the work of the revealer-prophet. Israel's life becomes entirely dependent upon the disclosure of God's will; for such disclosure it must rely upon its "eyes" and its "head" (the prophets; Isa. 29:10). And to Luke that disclosure was always attended by works, wonders, and signs. When those signs became apparent in the mission of John, Jesus, and the apostles, Israel was represented by the crowds who came out of Galilee and Judea to attend to their message and to be healed by their power.[20] To that embodiment of Consciousness B we now turn.

Before that transition, however, one final comment. I am quite aware that the effort in this chapter to make Luke's imagination and language intelligible will fall short of success. Our minds are too deeply controlled by Consciousness A to shift easily to this alien way of thinking and speaking. Nevertheless, a question posed by Karl Barth should continue to haunt us until our minds become more malleable:

> Why should not imagination grasp real history, or the poetry which is its medium be a representation of real history, of the kind of history which escapes ordinary analogies and cannot be verified historically, but is real history all the same?[21]

3

What I need I don't have
What I have I don't own
What I own I don't want
What I want, Lord, I don't know.[1]

THE NECESSITY OF
THE IMPOSSIBLE

I WANT NOW TO EXPLORE one other aspect of Consciousness B: its sense of tremendous need. It is true to say, I think, that every major world view available to men is powered by some implicit sense of man's deepest need. Whether or not this is true of all forms of Consciousness A, it is certainly true of Consciousness B; and the gateway to understanding it is the perception of this underlying urgency. The situations described in Luke 10 reflect this urgency. The seventy-two messengers will live as lambs surrounded by snapping wolves; those who hear them will be subject to the power of serpents and scorpions (that is, demons); every house and town will face the choice between Sodomic destruction and the peaceable kingdom. To be sure, this is hyperbolic language, but the hyperboles mirror the depths of struggle and anguish. In one way or another these images voice a single agonized human cry for deliverance.

Psalm 107

To catch the full force of that cry, let us look for a moment at Psalm 107, a typically biblical articulation of Israel's experience during many epochs. We have set out the core of this psalm in parallel columns (see p. 58f.). We should first notice the careful balancing of these four stanzas. Each stanza begins with a dramatic description of a crisis (lines 1); this description is amplified in lines 2 and 3, and is then summarized in lines 4, where it becomes clear that the persons described have passed beyond the point of self-help or even of deliverance by other men. With very few words the earlier lines picture different predicaments—wilderness, imprisonment, nausea, terror; but by the time the reader reaches lines 4 and 5 he becomes aware that a single plight is common to all. Line 5 can therefore be identical in all four stanzas: "They cried to the Lord in their trouble." The joining of these four groups in this unison cry to the Lord indicates a realized catholicity on the level of shared desperation. The forms of distress vary, yet all are embodied in the same cry. A similar catholicity is affirmed on the level of the divine response: "He delivered them from their distress." As recipients of this help, all four groups stand together. But to the poet this ecumenism of cry and reply does not eliminate the diversity in modes of liberation. Lines 7 and 8 show how God's intervention reversed the several specific forms of distress. Immediately, however, the various groups again join in a common refrain of gratitude (lines 9 and 10); in the latter two stanzas (lines 13 c,d and 14 c,d) the psalmist calls for the beneficiaries not only to thank God but to tell others of his help.

Many features of this ancient hymn are worth pondering. It exemplifies the biblical penchant for employing multiple parallels to suggest an unlimited range of particular circumstances and to stress simultaneously features which are common to all. The four stanzas can, by extension, be taken to cover all conceivable emergencies, yet they suggest that within them all men face a single recurring crisis. At the deepest levels of experience there is only one people and one

PSALM 107:4-32

vv.4–9	vv. 10–16

1a	Some wandered in desert wastes	1b	Some sat in darkness and gloom
2a	finding no way to a city to dwell in	2b	prisoners in affliction and in irons, for they had rebelled against the words of God, and spurned the counsel of the Most High
3a	hungry and thirsty	3b	Their hearts were bowed down with hard labor
4a	their soul fainted within them	4b	they fell down, with no one to help
5a	*Then they cried to the Lord in their trouble*	5b	*Then they cried to the Lord in their trouble*
6a	*and he delivered them from their distress*	6b	*and he delivered them from their distress*
7a	he led them by a straight way (cf. 2a)	7b	he brought them out of darkness and gloom (cf. 1b)
8a	till they reached a city to dwell in	8b	and broke their bonds asunder
9a	*Let them thank the Lord for his steadfast love*	9b	*Let them thank the Lord for his steadfast love*
10a	*for his wonderful works to the sons of men*	10b	*for his wonderful works to the sons of men*
11a	for he satisfies him who is thirsty (cf. 3a)	11b	For he shatters the doors of bronze (cf. 2b)
12a	and the hungry he fills with good things (cf. 3a)	12b	and cuts in two the bars of iron (cf. 2b)

PSALM 107:4-32

vv. 17–22	vv. 23–32

	Some went down to the sea in ships doing business on the great waters they saw the deeds of the Lord his wondrous works in the deep (cf. 10d)
	* For he commanded and raised the stormy wind
	** which lifted up the waves of the sea
1c Some were sick through their sinful ways	1d [Some] mounted up to heaven, they went down to the depths
2c and because of their iniquities suffered affliction	2d their courage melted away in their plight
3c they loathed any kind of food	3d they reeled and staggered like drunken men
4c and they drew near to the gates of death	4d and were at their wits' end
5c *Then they cried to the Lord in their trouble*	5d *Then they cried to the Lord in their trouble*
6c *and he delivered them from their distress*	6d *And he delivered them from their distress*
7c he sent forth his word and healed them (cf. 1c)	7d he made the storm be still (cf. d*)
8c and delivered them from destruction (cf. 4c)	8d and the waves of the sea were hushed (cf. d**)
9c *Let them thank the Lord for his steadfast love*	9d *Let them thank the Lord for his steadfast love*
10c *for his wonderful works to the sons of men*	10d *For his wonderful works to the sons of men*
13c And let them offer sacrifices of thanksgiving	13d Let them extol him in the congregation of the people
14c and tell of his deeds in songs of joy	14d and praise him in the assembly of the elders

God, one cry and one deliverance, one act of Thanksgiving and one song of joy.

We could extend the four stanzas to forty and yet employ the same chorus: "They cried . . . , and he delivered. . . ."

Each stanza also exemplifies the inclination to describe the conditions before and after God's action. This is done by employing a radical antithesis (for example, from "no way" to "a straight way" in lines 1a and 7a), a device not unlike that used in some of our modern advertising. In such descriptions there is a natural deftness in using external conditions to express internal emotions, without, however, separating objective from subjective features. Distress of soul is not disjoined from physical hunger. If one were to follow the modern tendency to separate the objective from the subjective components, he would have to give priority here to the subjective. Unity in the cry of distress is assumed to be more decisive than sharing life in the same prison or ship. The underlying assumption is that the hunger of the spirit, its longing for liberation and health and stability, is far more determinative than any external emergency. God's ability "to fill the hungry with good things" makes his deliverance far more enduring than if he were simply a heavenly CARE, Inc. But the very thrust of the four stanzas serves to prevent any facile disjunction between the two kinds of hunger, for example, physical versus spiritual, or literal versus figurative. Those who make that disjunction often suppose that the physical crisis is more terrible and less amenable to resolution than the spiritual. The psalmist would reverse such an evaluation. If we are to understand his thinking, we must follow his lead and evaluate all external situations as providing the context for man's agonized cry and God's gracious reply. In whatever crisis man stands there is the conjunction of both visible and invisible, or earthly and heavenly, realities. It is, of course, obvious that in the modern world, where most needs are described in terms of economic deficiencies to be met by political means, communities would no doubt produce a very different kind of psalm.[2]

Psalm 107 was quite clearly intended for use in the specific situation of worship; therefore we should not be surprised that it becomes most luminous when the covenant community unites in the praise of God and when God is "enthroned on" the praises of Israel. In such a context the psalm fulfills many liturgical functions; it is at once a confession of sin, a call to worship, a hymn of thanksgiving, and a testimony to the world. The speaker is the liturgist; the audience is Israel, gathered in the synagogue. Yet we must not isolate these liturgical functions from mundane involvements, for the psalm describes a wide range of nonliturgical crises, each of which evokes a cry for help. The synagogue is the place where world and worship are fused. So, too, the psalm bespeaks a communal situation where many men join in a single song of joy; yet the experienced desolations and restorations are also individualized. By way of vivid language, worship serves to activate the eyes and ears of each individual worshiper, so that he becomes newly aware of the depths of need in himself and aware of how this need unites him to his fellows.

We should also note the liturgical choice of tenses. Whereas in lines 1–8 verbs are used in the past tense and the language is retrospective, the tense of the address in lines 9–12 makes the action contemporaneous. With this shift from past tense to present, the community is seen to stand at the point of decision. In fact, the call to decide ("Let them thank the Lord"), which sounds much less urgent than the previous cry, actually creates the forward thrust of the entire psalm. The sequence of lines is such that "to give thanks," seemingly a quite innocuous act, receives an importance comparable to the preceding deliverance (like the action of the tenth leper in Luke 17:15–19, where gratitude is seen to be more redemptive even than being healed of leprosy). By this accent on present decision the psalm enables us to sift out two features of Consciousness B in which it differs sharply from Consciousness A.

1. Consciousness B views the external and internal definitions of the crisis as so interdependent that the intervention of God's grace instantaneously transforms the total situation from dereliction to plenitude.

2. Consciousness B views the two events, deliverance and thanksgiving, as so inseparable that only in the second event is the

meaning of the deliverance realized and made secure. In one of these events it is God who acts, in the other, man; yet the interaction of the two is so close that the story of the God worshiped comes to embrace the story of the worshipers. The perfect fusion of the two stories comes in worship which thus receives a cosmic scope.

We may well observe how this language is able to cope with this mysterious relation. It is a man, the liturgist, using a quite ordinary vocabulary, who recalls the four predicaments and who calls on the congregation to give thanks. Though the words are simple, they are weighted with profound meanings. So, too, are the words of his congregation, summoned to accept his memory as their own and, together with him, to offer their sacrifices of praise. Something significant happens at the junction of the two speeches, where the cry of men elicits God's reply. By his vocal address the liturgist sets up that encounter between these two voices of silence. His audible words are instruments of silent deliverance. That deliverance is consummated in the instant when men translate their silent deliverance into audible songs of joy. Without those joyful explosions, the whole sequence of events would have been aborted. In them the words of the liturgist and the *Amens* of the congregation become the media of fulfillment, the climax of the drama in four acts. It is possible, of course, to attribute too much creative power to this language, to the vocal sounds in and by themselves; but it is folly to ignore their strategic role, whether one thinks of them as words of men or as the Word of God. A text of this kind offers an excellent example of the hermeneutical principle stressed by Paul Ricoeur, and noted in chapter 1, that the text points beyond itself to a mode of being-in-the-world and that to understand the text the reader must move in that direction. The original psalmist so deftly articulated the dereliction of all congregations that in each congregation, whether ancient or modern, the worshiper is aided in voicing his own cry for deliverance and his own song of joy to the same God, in this way celebrating the reality of creation and redemption.

In speaking of the various functions of liturgical language we should not overlook the large repertoire of images used by the psalmist. Each of the four stanzas utilizes an extensive constellation of allusions, rugged and elemental in character. The grim picture of isolation in the desert without road or shelter is replaced by that of travel on a straight road to a hospitable city where hunger, thirst, and fatigue are replaced by food, drink, and renewed strength. In the second stanza multiple forms of frustration are called to mind by the description of hard labor, the darkness of affliction, the "doors of bronze" and "bars of iron." In the second and third stanzas the dereliction is explicitly traced to sin against God, which, by the logic of parallel construction, can be assumed to be present in the other two stanzas as well. This implies, in turn, that the act of deliverance required in every case the forgiveness of this sin. This is surely the case in the third stanza, where conditions of sickness, nausea, and death (due to sin, 1c, 2c) are overcome by God's word of healing. Thus already in the psalm we meet the thought pattern that would become so common in the Gospels, a pattern which correlates sickness with sin as the burden of man's cry, and which links God's word of forgiveness to the cure of illness.

There are at least two innovations in the fourth stanza. Its greater length is presumably due to the need to introduce the storm at sea, to suggest the power of the winds and waves to instill terror. The onset of the storm, together with the subsequent stillness, is here attributed to God, possibly indicating that in the first three stanzas as well, God's hand might be discerned in the creation of the very emergencies from which men cry for relief. However that may be, analysis of the four stanzas strengthens the conclusion that they all describe a single plight on the part of God's people, one capable of being described by an extensive glossary of metaphors. Whoever would grasp the character of Consciousness B must have an intuitive empathy for these metaphors as descriptive of his own predicament, or he must create analogous images more indigenous to his own vocabulary.

DERELICTION IN LUKE

If we examine Luke's summaries of those whom Jesus helped, there can be little doubt of his empathy with the psalmist. Here are four of those summaries:[3]

4:18	6:20–22	7:22	14:21
the poor	the poor	the blind	the poor
the captives	the hungry	the lame	the maimed
the blind	the mourners	the lepers	the blind
the oppressed	the persecuted	the deaf	the lame
		the dead	
		the poor	

Common to all four lists is *the poor,* a category which appears in an important position, either first or last. Although we may tend to view these as different groups of people, Luke probably had in mind one group whose dereliction could be described in these various ways, as is clearly the case in 6:20–22. Each list has a mixture of categories which seems to modern readers somewhat incongruous: the physically ill are listed with the economically poor and the socially ostracized. However, this very mixture serves to indicate what is the common denominator in all cases: these people all know the sense of futility, incapacity, and helplessness. All must rely upon some source outside themselves for any alleviation of their distress. As in the great hymn of defiance and thanksgiving, the Magnificat, the four lists assume that these people all know the kind of weakness that can be remedied only by intervention from heaven.

> "He has shown strength with his arm,
> he has scattered the proud in the
> imagination of their hearts,
> he has put down the mighty from
> their thrones,
> and exalted those of low degree;
> he has filled the hungry with good
> things,
> and the rich he has sent empty away" (1:51–53).

In other briefer texts, where Luke as an editor summarizes such interventions from heaven, Jesus' help is recorded as extending to two groups, either the sick and the demon-possessed (4:40; 6:18; 9:1; 10:8, 17) or the sick and the sinful (5:17, 31). As we have already observed, this last passage (5:31) reflects the assumption that sickness and demon-possession are related to sin and that therefore the act of forgiveness becomes often an act of healing or exorcism. To unclean spirits Luke attributed various ailments, sometimes undefined (4:33; 8:27) and sometimes defined: dumbness (11:14) or paralysis (13:11). In other instances Luke does not specify the work of unclean spirits: paralysis (5:18), withered hand (6:6), dropsy (14:2), leprosy (17:12), blindness (18:35), and death (7:12; 8:49). We note that all the items as listed in 7:22, except deafness, are illustrated elsewhere in the Gospel by stories of specific cures. Moreover, all the emergencies described in Psalm 107 are paralleled in Luke, including even the terror prompted by the typhoon (8:22–25). Luke was no more inclined than the psalmist to separate the objective from the subjective factors, a feature which baffles interpreters. In the Gospel as in the psalm, the stories of Jesus' aid (or God's) are told in such a way as to underscore the contrast between the situations before and after the experience of deliverance. Before divine relief comes, men are subject to intense guilt, isolation, lostness, hunger, hostility, poverty. Afterward they express awe, joy, and gratitude. Basically the same conditions characterize the stories in Acts, where relief is mediated by the word and work of the apostles. This fact indicates that we would be quite wrong to attribute the miracles of the Gospel simply to the desire to prove the unique and exclusive power of Jesus as Messiah. As Luke 10 shows, this writer wanted to show how the Word of God was creative of a single community, bound together by its need and God's help, his gift and its gratitude, with Jesus and his messengers presented as mediators of the same deliverance.

Luke believed that the constituency of this community had corresponded to the conscious intention of Jesus: not the mighty, but the meek; not the well, but the sick; not the righteous, but sinners (5:31–32). Their love became proportionate to their prior dereliction (7:43). The stories told of one disciple after another disclosed the character of the entire church: Simeon (2:25ff.), Anna (2:36ff.), the praying publican (18:13), the self-effacing widow (21:2ff.). Members of the church were described in the four beatitudes of 6:20–22 and in the account of the little flock who had traded all they possessed for treasure in heaven (12:22–34). All were poor, not only in the sense of Barnabas' action (Acts 4:36f.) but more significantly in the sense of total dependence on God's help. Luke used the term *the poor* with a force it had acquired in the Old Testament prophets to connote "the hopelessness of ever gaining God's salvation."[4] To proclaim good news to them was to announce that God had made possible what had earlier been impossible (Lk. 1:37, 49; 18:27). Later developments had been anticipated in the pilot journey of the seventy-two in Luke 10, where the impossible had become possible (10:21–24), an image connoting a miraculous victory over weakness, guilt, sickness, captivity. To trust wholly in God's possibility enabled the "babes" to be cured, liberated, and fed. Thus the stories of the Gospel conveyed the paradox of deliverance in a way comparable to the litany of Psalm 107. The language of psalm and Gospel echoed the awareness that life in this particular desert was worse than life in any conceivable Sahara, and that the gift of life in this city was preferable to life in any conceivable Shangri-La. The use of each hyperbole simply attested the strategic importance of such evaluations, indigenous to Consciousness B but quite alien to Consciousness A.[5]

THE IMPOSSIBLE POSSIBILITY

Let us take seriously the conception of impossibility as the burden of the one cry (Ps. 107, lines 4). It is implicit in Luke's insight into all the categories to whom Jesus announced the good news in Luke 4:18. Consider, for example, the group whom he calls the poor. What ranges of need did Luke visualize in that image? There are various interlocking levels. First there are the immediate economic and social accompaniments of poverty: the poor have no money to buy the food, clothing, and shelter they need in order to survive and to be fully accepted by their fellows. Second is their inability ever to improve their status or to achieve equality and justice; the odds are permanently against them. Third is the perennial failure of society to redress the grievances of the poor and to provide instruments of justice in marketplace or dwelling or law courts. Benevolence is not enough and justice is unattainable; for every step forward toward more just institutions, society appears to slip two steps backward, steadily widening the differential between classes. Fourth, this failure to secure a just distribution of economic resources becomes symbolic of all human efforts within the range of human history to achieve any lasting alleviation of distress. History comes to be experienced as the mother who devours her own children, or as the box of puzzles with a lost key. In being abandoned to the power of their enemies, the "poor" experience the apparent death of God, the inaccessibility of his forgiveness and the unreality of his peace. As T. W. Manson wrote in a previous Shaffer lecture:

> The culture promises nothing for their future; if they have a future it will be a gift to them, and a gift unlike the prerequisites which society could give if it would.[6]

So much for the situation of the poor. An equally broad band of experience is connoted by the other images of distress: demon-possession, persecution, captivity, hunger, leprosy, widowhood, death. When Luke quotes from the promises of Isaiah in 4:16–21, 6:20–23, and 7:22, he uses multiple metaphors to designate a single human reality, as in the Tannaitic aphorism, "Four are compared with a dead man: the lame, the blind, the leper and the childless."[7] When people cry for help from Jesus or his messengers, they are crying for the impossible; when that cry evokes the offer of God's kingdom, that offer transforms the impossibility into a possibility. Together, the cry and response become a mysterious and miraculous sign of "the redemption of Israel." This is why the fulfillment of the promise of a prophet like Moses should lead to an eruption of signs comparable to those which marked the Exodus from Egypt.

To be sure, the very mention of the miraculous provokes the shock of disbelief among modern readers, and this shock recurs in almost every paragraph Luke wrote. The work of Luke's prophets was marked by a series of signs and wonders which were attributed to God's power and understood as evidence of the approach of God's kingdom. In his commissioning of his advance scouts, for example, Jesus gave two commands in the same breath: "Heal the sick and say to them, 'The kingdom of God has come near to you' " (10:9). This deed and this word correspond precisely to the double focus of Jesus' work in Nazareth (4:16–30). The interdependence of the two was as integral to the prophetic consciousness as it is unintelligible to the modern. What is a sign of heaven's nearness in one is evidence of a charlatan's trick in the other. Consciousness A insists on transporting the sign into its own thought world where it becomes a contravention of natural law, impossible by definition. Here the sign can only delude the unwary. Whatever it may now signify, whether it arouses credulity or scepticism, the meaning is distorted and it no longer signifies what it did as a feature of Consciousness B. Given the character of the two mentalities, the confrontation aroused by the mention of miracles can neither be avoided nor resolved. This the history of exegesis makes clear.[8] It may, however, help us to understand this impasse if we look first at the Lucan picture of those who are healed and then at his picture of the healers.

We have already looked at the various descriptions of the forms of dereliction and have noted how they all express an extremity of need and a unity among suppliants at the point of deepest urgency, where the impossibility of help impels a cry for deliverance. This sense of impotence triggers a positive response to the announcement that divine power is at long last available. We should now go further to observe how Luke views those who come to Jesus or to his disciples to be healed. That view is conveyed in the editorial introductions to various narratives and it can be reliably recaptured.

These Lucan introductions indicate that to Jesus the ultimate concern was to reach the people (*laos*), that is, the covenant community, Israel. The stories in Acts speak of this community in various terms: "my people" (7:34), "children of Abraham" (13:26), "dwelling of David" (15:16). It is normal for Luke to think of this community as the initial and ultimate audience for God's messengers, whether John the Baptist (Acts 13:24) or the apostles (Acts 3:12f.). The first step in the process of bringing this audience to repentance and faith is for them to hear the Word and to see the signs (Acts 5:12–16). It is in the presence of this *laos* as a whole that the signs are wrought (Acts 6:8). As in Acts, the Gospel also assumes that this people constitutes the goal of the combined vocation of preaching and healing. In their presence Jesus had vindicated his prophetic vocation by his powerful deeds and words (Lk. 24:19). It is often implied that, when this *laos* appeared on the same stage with the Twelve, Jesus was training the latter to minister to the former (Lk. 6:17; 7:1; 9:13; 20:45).[9]

In both of Luke's volumes the *laos* was often represented by the crowd (*ochlos*) which became the immediate audience of the apostles or of Jesus. Their action was often described as a coming out to hear the word and to see the signs, and perchance to be healed of their infirmities (Lk. 5:15). They were potential believers who usually spoke together as a chorus. Their coming out indicated an eagerness to learn what they must do to be saved, but in hearing the word they also needed to beware of *how* they heard (Lk. 8:8). Hearing had to be followed by the costly obedience and self-denial required of all disciples. Theirs was the dereliction conveyed by such images as we have surveyed: hunger, leprosy, paralysis, death. The word which they came out to hear, the signs which they came out to see, constituted the impossible possibility of which Luke speaks throughout. Coming out into the "wilderness" as representatives of Israel, they became the source from which Jesus enlisted disciples, men and women who could testify both to blindness and to the gift of sight.

There is no doubt that, according to Luke, the prophets whom Jesus appointed had to share in the derelictions found in their audience. Neither wise nor powerful, they were infants. Only so could they become the conduit for heavenly wisdom and power to those who, like themselves, had no resources of their own. This is the basic logic of Luke 10, where the event of revelation/healing moved from Jesus to the seventy-two and then to the crowds of helpless seekers. In this strange vocation speakers and listeners alike had to declare bankruptcy with regard to visible means of support, to recognize a daily dependence upon gifts of bread from heaven. Theologians of hope have recently been stressing the dependence of beggars upon such gifts. For instance, Jürgen Moltmann distinguishes between two futures. One represents the imposition of present conditions upon the future, a process that is "always conservative." The other future begins by changing the present, and can only come to the suffering.[10] If, with Jeremias we conclude that "salvation is destined only for beggars and sinners,"[11] we must also conclude that this salvation can be promised only by prophets who have humbled themselves beneath those beggars and sinners.

This logic as expressed by the impossibility-possibility dialectic pervades Luke's thought and therefore his vocabulary as well. We should sense its presence everywhere in his description of the work of prophets. In our lexicon many terms have lost their prophetic content which in his lexicon conveyed a full measure of revelatory power: the word of God, preaching, the gospel, witness, wisdom, salvation, the Holy Spirit. Each of these terms referred, from one angle or another, to the traffic between heaven and the helpless, from the realm of future grace to the realm of present impotence, to the folk in the crowds who had come out to hear and to be healed. The word came with authority, and these hungry and lost souls recognized that authority.

If the authority had followed the patterns of "the rulers of this age," it would not have met their needs: these poor could not be helped by the authority of the rich, whose philanthropies would only have increased their dependence. These sinners could not profit from the righteous, nor these sick from the healthy. They had ailments that could only respond to the ministrations of others who were themselves wounded, to physicians who could not heal themselves. In short, these folk could be helped only by a reversal in the direction from which their help would come, that is, from those who in recognizing a greater impotence had also received a sign of God's power.

This same logic discloses the decisive importance of the prophet-revealer. Apart from his word, his sign, and his interpretation of the sign, the possibility of help for the helpless remained theoretical. God required some spokesmen to announce his answer to the long years of pleading, to declare the "today" in which the promised help had come near. The heavenly decision remained "really invisible," therefore the word of a revealer was required; the action of God had become "invisibly real," therefore the revealer must interpret the sign and his interpretation must elicit faith that the impossible had in fact become possible and that the kingdom of God had drawn near. From this standpoint alone can we understand how Consciousness B assumed that the prophet-revealer would work wonders of liberation and that such wonders would be interpreted as verifying his heavenly authority. As Luke tells the story of the first missions, both Jesus and the crowds expected the envoys to work wonders (9:40; 10:8–20); the envoys rejoiced on learning that in the flight of demons such an expectation had been fulfilled.

We make one further observation regarding the logic implicit in the impossible-possibility of help given to the helpless. This logic made necessary certain requirements of the prophet-revealer-healers if they were to reveal *this* heaven and to channel *this* kind of authority to the crowds. The logic required that the prophet who was Son of man must suffer, be betrayed, be rejected, be killed, and be raised from the dead by God. Only then could he dispense the power needed by his delegates. And this truth is a ground for understanding one of the central motifs in the Gospel portrait of Jesus. The same logic required of those delegates that they receive that power by a similar path. Only so can we fully understand why Jesus told them:

> "Take nothing for your journey, no staff, no bag, nor bread, nor money; and do not have two tunics" (9:3).

> "I send you out as lambs in the midst of wolves. Carry no purse, no bag, no sandals; and salute no one on the road" (10:3–4).

The context of these commands implies that this manner of life was viewed as essential to the preaching of the kingdom, to the ability to dispense peace, to the healing of the sick, and to the call for repentance in houses and cities. That Luke sensed this connection is also implied in a later reminder of these very instructions:

"When I sent you out with no purse or bag or sandals, did you lack anything? They said 'Nothing' " (22:35).[12]

We may surmise various reasons for such stern and binding instructions. Why did Jesus compel his authorized messengers to adopt the life of wandering beggars? To vindicate their capacity for sacrifice and self-denial? That seems to be part of the truth, but only part. To warn all his followers against wealth and reliance on money as the root of all evil? That attitude may well have been present. To support the Acts picture of the ideal Christian community in which all members would contribute their resources and from which they would receive whatever they needed? That, too, is characteristic of Luke's emphasis. None of these, however, is quite adequate. In this case Luke was dealing neither with the general demands on all disciples, the common lifestyle of the Jerusalem church nor the insidiously corrupting influence of wealth, but with qualifications which would enable these delegates to heal the sick and to preach good news to the poor. That task required that they be as helpless as lambs in a pack of wolves. It required that they learn, by having nothing, to lack nothing (22:35). Only as beggars without visible resources could they convey invisible resources to other beggars. Only by renouncing all forms of earthly authority which operate from above downward could they release men from demonic captivity. Only by becoming helpless could they help other helpless. The resources of heaven, which were accessible to babes and which could be relayed to them only by prophets whose authority exemplified Principle B, produced signs fully consistent with those resources. This must be firmly kept in mind whenever Gospel miracles are under discussion; otherwise we mistake both their character and significance.

It is clear that attitudes toward the miraculous provide an excellent index of the contrasts between the two world views. Let us first describe the cluster of attitudes typical of Consciousness A. Within this context, miracles are usually defined as events that contravene natural laws. It will be assumed that those laws are well known and that the more spectacular the collision with such laws, the more miraculous the event. Great weight will be attached to the question "Did such an event actually take place?" Accordingly, great importance will be attributed to the objective evidences supporting claims that it did. Physical blindness will be considered more terrible and incorrigible than spiritual blindness, and its cure more difficult. A proof of cure will be required before one believes in it. The power to heal the sick will be considered more impressive than the power to forgive sins; it will be more difficult to believe in the raising of the dead than to believe that the kingdom of God has drawn near. The prestige of a religious leader will often depend upon the stupendous character of the miracles credited to him. In all this, it should be evident that this cluster of attitudes is more deeply rooted and more determinative of a world view than formal religious attachments. Some who hold this cluster of attitudes will reject out of hand all New Testament references to signs and wonders. Others, however, may accept many of those signs, but this acceptance will not produce any basic changes in their pictures of the universe. Like the Pharisees of old, they may not contest the actuality of Jesus' cures, but neither will they experience that revolution in world views which signals the dawning of the kingdom of God.

From all this, Consciousness B, as illustrated by Luke, is radically different. To the evangelist the invasion of the powers of the kingdom marked the greater change, with the healing of the sick a secondary sign of that change. It was the gospel preached to the poor that effected their liberation; it was by faith in that gospel that men were cured of all manner of impotence and hopelessness, with repercussions in manifold kinds of psychic and somatic release. The announcement of the conquest of demons triggered such explosive hopes that men's physical powers were renewed and they were impelled toward achievements which till then had been quite impossible. These signs disclosed the nearness of the kingdom, the authority of Jesus and his delegates, the fall of Satan from heaven, and God's immediate intervention in the affairs of Bethsaida and Capernaum. The signs transformed the situation at a level deeper than the felt needs of individual blind men. Once men believed in the actuality of this dawn, belief in the actuality of exorcisms was easy—as easy as belief that Pharisees could also cast out demons, without, however, matching the significance of Jesus' exorcisms. The stories of Jesus' mighty works are, of course, later than the events themselves. They are

> complicated structures of reflection to which much has contributed: memories of scenes in the life of Jesus, experiences that the disciples had with Jesus before and after his death, the immediate needs of the primitive church; and all this is interpreted within the frame of the prophets' messianic experience of history and is poetically intensified into a symbolic and expressive story.[13]

The urgent question posed by these stories in Luke was whether or not the age of which they were the signs had actually dawned. The emergence of faith in that dawn was more impressive in that it was more difficult than belief in the actuality of healing (a condition which may again have become true in our own day). Other definitions of miracles did not really require the intervention of the word of the Messiah or of the prophets, but only the demonstrable power of a magician or exorcist. But in Luke's conception of the human predicament, the coming of a prophet was necessary if there were to be such a channeling of divine power as to mark the descent of God's kingdom from heaven to earth. Such a prophet would both produce signs and himself become "a sign that was spoken against." Luke 10 records those signs in terms of power over demons, serpents, and human "wolves." This fact means that we are still within the circle of reasoning that we noted in Psalm 107:

> They cried to the Lord in their trouble,
> He delivered them from their distress,

though we have moved into a period when such deliverance was the work of prophets uttering the "word of the Lord."

The essential matter in this discussion of miracle is threefold: (1) Luke lived in a world where the need for salvation was conjoined to the work of prophets, presenting signs of their heavenly authority. (2) That vocation included the task of raising the consciousness of Israel to the point of recognizing God's presence in those prophetic signs. (3) Even more essential was the fact that, by his compassion for the helpless, Jesus "rendered every previous idea of God obsolete."[14] It was to this new disclosure of God's power that the signs and wonders must be traced, for here the focus shifts "not only to the oppressed and the lost, but in them to the insignificant. . . . Jesus himself is present among the helpless as an element in their lowliness, standing in darkness not in splendor. . . . The unexpectedness of finding the Redeemer as a helpless Child communicates itself constantly to Christian love."[15] It was the therapeutic power of messianic suffering, or rather God's power released through that suffering, which distinguished exorcisms and cures in the New Testament from ancient Hellenistic wonder stories as well as from modern faith healing by revivalist preachers.[16] In short, we will not enter Luke's world without grasping the fact that healing and revealing were twin aspects of a single prophetic vocation. "Heal the sick . . . and say to them, 'The kingdom of God has come near to you' " (10:9). And we will not grasp how healing meant revealing, and how revealing meant healing, without grasping the mystery of how weakness had become the channel of God's power.

We have now reached a vantage point from which to scan the ideas developed in Part One. We started with the aim of making more intelligible to modern readers the kinds of prophetic language which are to be found in the New Testament, using the writing of Luke as a test case. Selecting for analysis a specific episode (10:1–24), we located eight salient features of Luke's outlook which readers find especially difficult to fathom. Of those eight we placed three clusters under close scrutiny: attitudes toward authority, toward heaven, and toward wonderful signs.

Still remaining unexamined are five constellations of attitudes: the pervasive activity of God, the invasive movement of his kingdom, the mediating roles of the Holy Spirit, the hostility between lambs and wolves, and the overarching warfare between God and Satan. Although each of these clusters merits separate study, we shall not undertake to do so here. For one thing, adequate space is lacking, for to deal thoroughly with them would require too long a volume on Lucan theology. For another thing, we shall be dealing with many of these ideas, albeit obliquely, in Part Two. In any case, it is much better if each reader, operating at his own tempo and on his own initiative, explores the other features of Consciousness B. Once freed from the narrow restrictive thought world of Consciousness A and aware of the more spacious and more human world of Luke, he will need less external guidance.

For instance, each of our three chapters suggests directions in which to go in tracing Luke's attitudes toward God. Where do we find this God? Wherever this unique kind of authority is operating. His throne is to be located in this particular kind of heaven, where everything earthly has its origin, sustenance, and goal. His power is to be discerned in these kinds of signs and wonders as they bring liberation to these particular captives. When our eyes have become accustomed to the lights and shadows of this terrain of thought, we can begin to understand the profound truth in the statement that only this Son could disclose this Father (Lk. 10:22). We can also begin to understand where Luke located the boundaries between the kingdom of this God and the kingdom of his archenemy, the power of darkness. And why Luke believed that wolves would attack any lambs who came proclaiming this particular peace, healing the sick with this medicine, and joining this prophet on his journey to Jerusalem. Here is a vast world of experience, to be entered into by babes to whom the Holy Spirit grants a vision of things which "prophets and kings have longed to see."

Much more could well be added here, but it is time to turn to our second major objective: a clearer conception of the prophetic vocation as Luke understood it. Since he expressed no general idea of such a vocation, but simply told the stories of particular prophets, we will review his stories of three generations of charismatic leaders: John the Baptist, Jesus, and the messengers Jesus called to continue his work. Thus far it is their language that we have tried to make intelligible; we now attempt to do the same thing for their vocation. Thus far we have positioned ourselves as the first readers of Luke-Acts; now we will position ourselves as auditors of these seers and exorcists. As no one today is writing in a language similar to Luke's, so also no one today has a vocation exactly the same as those healer-revealers. Consequently the vocation is as difficult to comprehend as the language, perhaps even more difficult. In any case, I am convinced that no one can truly break into Luke's universe of discourse without listening to this prophetic succession. Thus Part Two of this study becomes a necessary extension of Part One.

Part Two

THE PROPHETIC VOCATION

4

Repentance was hardest for the pious man, because he was separated from God not by crude sins but by his piety. Nothing separates a man from God so radically as self-assured piety. [1]

JOHN AS A PROPHET LIKE ELIJAH

At this point the target of our study shifts, from the more generalized consciousness to the more specific vocation. What we have called Consciousness B can refer to two different things: to that universe of thought on the part of a prophet's audience which makes his message and work intelligible to them; or to that orientation on the part of the prophet himself which is built into his vocation under God. These two things are interrelated but yet distinct. It is the former that we have dubbed Consciousness B, with Luke as an exemplar. He did not speak of himself as recipient of a special vocation but only as a transmitter of prophetic traditions. In turning to the analysis of such vocations, therefore, we will discontinue our use of the contrast between Consciousness A and B, although the discerning reader may notice how that contrast becomes all the sharper as we consider the inner structure and dynamics of the vocation of specific prophets.

Our central concern will be Luke's portrait of Jesus as one prophet in a succession of prophets. This feature does not of course exhaust Luke's ways of picturing Jesus, but I think this way has a strategic importance which has too long been neglected. In their effort to stress the uniqueness of Jesus, modern Christians often isolate him from predecessors and successors. Not so, Luke. To him this prophet belonged within a series of prophets; this succession helped to clarify and to reinforce the vocation of each member. By reviewing the work of John as a prophet like Elijah, and the work of the apostles as prophets like Jesus, we may recover many valuable clues to the distinctive vocation of Jesus. That, at least, is a conviction which will be tested in what follows.

We will still rely of course upon the reporting of the author whom we call Luke. It is inevitable that as a reporter he should fall short of providing the kind of accuracy and completeness which might be desired. He was dependent upon traditions relayed to him by others. Even when he had the benefit of direct observation of a prophet's work, his third-person account is bound to differ from that of other observers, not to speak of the prophet's own firsthand testimony. (Compare, for example, Paul's own references to the origin of his own vocation in Gal. 1:11 ff. with Luke's three accounts of that call in Acts 9;22;26.) Third-person accounts are subject to various kinds of romantic idealization, as the events celebrated move into the more distant past. It is easy for the reporter, in stressing the actualities of inner experiences, to place the accent on external marvels; how else can he do justice to the power with which "the word of the Lord" made its impact? We should not treat Luke's narratives as immune to errors of fact or judgment; they represent neither the firsthand testimony of the apostles nor the unanimous verdict of his Christian colleagues.

On the other hand, we should not minimize Luke's own implicit claims. He believed firmly that all believers had received the gift of the Holy Spirit. He would have agreed with Paul that no one can avow the Lordship of Christ except as a recipient of that gift (I Cor. 12:3). There is every reason to share the attitude expressed in the earliest "prologue" to the Gospel that Luke was "a disciple of the apostles" and "full of the Holy Spirit."[2] He may not have viewed all believers as prophets in the narrower sense, but he clearly expected every congregation to have sufficient gifts of the Spirit to comprehend what the Spirit was saying to it through the prophets. He seemed to have viewed the church as a group of charismatic communities linked together by itinerant charismatic leaders, "eyewitnesses and ministers of the word" (Lk. 1:2). The vocational compulsions of each prophet were probably so mysterious and powerful as to test the spiritual capacities of his audience; in fact, it would be strange indeed if each audience fully understood the thrust of each message and sign. Even so, the gift of interpretation seems to have been present from the earliest days (e.g., I Cor. 14:26–33), and we can rely within certain limits on the competence of reporters like Luke to give us accurate profiles of prophets at work.[3]

The Gospel in the Light of Acts

It is in some ways easier to recapture Luke's notion of the prophets than the notions of Matthew or Mark, because Luke wrote not one volume but two. The second volume often enables us to discern clues to his perspectives in the first. Many scholars seek to recover Luke's theology almost wholly by the use of a synoptic harmony and by a careful scrutiny of every variant between the Lucan text and an earlier source, whether Mark or a conjectured text of Q. Often scholars assume that when Luke wrote he had immediately before him those two earlier texts and that virtually every variation discloses a conscious alteration in the direction of rejecting a theological point made by the earlier writer in the interest of a contrary point which Luke wished to make. A comparative study of this kind has many merits, but I believe that in his own mind when Luke was writing the Gospel he was not so much revising earlier documents to conform to his own theological notions as composing the first of two volumes which would be read together by the same readers. The interdependence of these two volumes is such that the purposes of volume one can be most clearly discerned by observing the contents and sequences of volume two. In the words of W.C. van Unnik: "Acts was not an afterthought or a second, independent work on another topic; Luke-Acts was well planned as one work in two volumes."[4]

Luke's literary design may be detected in the way in which he begins and ends the two volumes; here the role of charismatic ministry receives a central place. In the Gospel preface the author acknowledges his own dependence upon "those who from the beginning were eyewitnesses and ministers of the word." In the Gospel conclusion, the vocation of those eyewitnesses is confirmed by the Risen Lord who promises to send them power from on high, enabling them to carry his message to all nations. The introduction to the second volume repeats what had been the burden of the closing verses of the first: Jesus' mandate to his messengers, the reinterpretation for them of his passion, his definition of the scope of their mission ("the end of the earth"), and his promise that they would receive power through baptism by the Spirit. Through them Jesus would continue to do what he had begun to do before his execution.[5] Ever since his account of the baptism of John, Luke had had his eye on the preparation of the apostles as prophetic see-ers and say-ers.

This continuity in perspective is reflected in the vocabulary and imagery which bind the two volumes together: the word of God, the Spirit, the angel of the Lord, preaching, witnessing, teaching, repentance, baptism, forgiveness, signs and wonders, suffering and glory. Volume one begins with the whole people being baptized with water; volume two with that same *laos* baptized with the Spirit. The rejection of this same Spirit links the rulers of the Nazareth synagogue in Luke 4 to the leaders of the Roman Jews in Acts 28. From first to last there is an unbroken chain of angelic and human revealers and messengers, whose word was rejected or accepted, each rejection and acceptance marking the fulfillment of old promises and the issuance of new. When one searches for a word indigenous to Luke's lexicon to describe this continuous chain of mediators between heaven and earth, the word best qualified to point to the chain of divine callings and human vocations is the word *prophet*. This word recurs in four major contexts: the prophet who came in the spirit and power of Elijah, the prophet whom God raised up like Moses, the apostolic prophets who worked in the spirit and power of Jesus, and the community in which *all* were baptized with the same

Spirit and *all* prophesied (Acts 2:17; 10:44; 19:6). I am convinced that this prophetic succession was more decisive for Luke than any "apostolic succession." I am also convinced that we may find here many neglected clues to the vocation of Jesus.

In taking this theme I acknowledge indebtedness to two cherished colleagues, Paul Schubert and Nils Dahl. Paul Schubert convincingly established the centrality and significance in Luke-Acts of the proof-from-prophecy theology.[6] This thesis has been ably supported by Nils Dahl, who writes, "I know of no other recapitulation of biblical history in which the idea of successive fulfillments of prophecy is so prominent."[7] Each promise in the history of Israel is definitely though partially fulfilled, and each such fulfillment gives way to a new promise.

At the moment I suggest two modifications in this thesis. Instead of *prophecy* and fulfillment I want to accent *the prophets* and fulfillment. Luke understood the Spirit which fulfilled one prophet's word as operating through a prophet who succeeded him and in whom God carried out his pledge. Furthermore, I propose that we concentrate here on three specific and connected stages in the succession of prophets: John the Baptist, Jesus, the Twelve. For Luke, Jesus' vocation presupposed that of John and predetermined that of his apostles. Each of these three stages possessed its own unique features. But God as the ultimate **source** of the promise and the people of God as the ultimate *audience* remained the same.

We will devote the remainder of this chapter to two matters: Luke's attitude toward the prophetic vocation in general and his portrait of John's work in particular. Both these matters have strategic implications for Luke's understanding of Jesus.

LUKE'S GALLERY OF PROPHETS

Although the Evangelist was primarily concerned with the period of prophecy beginning with John, this period was linked to prophets who reached back to the very beginning of things. The earliest prophet cited is Abel (Lk. 11:51) whose death disclosed a continuity in rejection and suffering that began with "the foundation of the world." Standing at the point where God called into existence a chosen race is the prophet Abraham (Acts 3:25; 7:2–8; Lk. 1:55; 12:28). Standing at the point where God sealed the Sinai covenant with Israel in the first Exodus is the prophet Moses. Standing at the inauguration of the kingship is the prophet David. The same chain included, of course, Samuel, Elijah, and Elisha, along with those whose prophecies had become embodied in written form: Isaiah, Malachi, Zechariah, Joel, Jonah. All these had roles in Luke's scenario. Luke would fully endorse Isaiah's description of prophets as the "eyes" and the "head" of God's people (Isa. 29:10).

This very inclusiveness means that a vast variety of spiritual gifts was designated by the same word; this variety, in turn, makes it virtually impossible to define the vocation by a single set of job specifications. It is difficult to sort out the elements common to the vocations of Abel, David, Isaiah, Paul, Agabus. Moreover, from generation to generation God kept the anointing in his own hands; ignoring popular expectations, he rather chose spokesmen who would defy conventional patterns and confound the professionals. The needs of Israel were endlessly diverse; the functions of prophecy were equally pluriform. Some needs were limited and temporary, others were decisive and permanent.

When Luke spoke of the prophetic role in his own day he included an even wider range of emergencies and purposes. Such a purpose was the disclosure to Paul, at a single point in time, of the trouble which he would face in going to Jerusalem, or the disclosure to the congregation in Antioch of the impending shortage of food for the brothers in Jerusalem. Sometimes heaven's guidance was directed to the selection of an itinerary: should the apostle enter Asia or should he leave Corinth? Within the agenda of a worship assembly came opportunities for various members to express various gifts of the Spirit, including prophecy (Acts 2:1–47; 19:6). On occasion, the gift would be expended in a moment or two, yet the same gift might extend over a lifetime. On occasion the audience would be a single individual, or it might be the whole *laos,* and the gift would serve to seal an abiding covenant with it. When Luke drew examples from Israel's past he naturally selected pivotal figures: Lot or Solomon or Jonah. In dealing with the present he believed in the prophethood of all believers, since all were baptized into the one Spirit and the one name; yet at the same time he believed in the distinctive authority of the missionary prophets. All these differences must be respected, yet they do not prevent us from drawing a profile of the work of those prophets whose assignments were most inclusive and permanent. Such a profile should be broad enough to cover many examples, yet narrow enough to fit specific men and women. In constructing it we should focus on specific texts in which Luke uses the term prophet and on specific persons whom he explicitly recognizes as such. Yet we should also reckon with the fact that prophetic activity may be in view when the word itself is absent. Recognizing the difficulties and dangers in reducing so many variables to a common abstract pattern, we yet believe that it is helpful to visualize a vocation characterized by the following ten features. [8]

1. *The prophet is a revealer,* called to stand in the counsels of the Most High and to disclose to men God's invisible will and purposes for them. Conscious of standing as a go-between on the frontier between heaven and earth, [9] the prophet is often overwhelmed by awesome privilege and fearsome responsibility. There were conventional ways of describing this boundary situation: Luke used rather bold technicolor—the opening of heaven, the descent of angels or the ascent of the prophet, the activity of the Holy Spirit, the hand of God, dreams and visions. The kind and degree of ecstasy which the prophet experienced was hard to anticipate and impossible to prescribe; and yet the conscious experience of a divine summons to serve as revealer seems to have been an essential common feature.

2. *The prophet is a see-er,* whose experience often involved a gift of vision, a second sight. He became a witness induced to say, "I saw. . . ." What had earlier been invisible to him, what was still invisible to others, had become visible to him. Sometimes this referred to the secrets of men's hearts, sometimes to the secrets of heaven, and sometimes to both in conjunction. On seeing the invisible

world, he recognized an immediate and significant nexus between the invisible purpose of God and the decisions confronting his audience. The gift of prophecy thus entailed gifts of insight and foresight, in which the basic metaphor of seeing functioned as the linguistic corollary to the divine act of unveiling.

3. *The prophet is an auditor,* a listener, whose vision was normally associated with audition. It was assumed that the see-er became a hearer, impelled to say, "I heard. . . ." The voice which spoke to him commanded him to speak, although on occasion the command to keep silent might itself be a form of communication. What the prophet heard was inaudible to others, yet through him it became audible as the voice of God confronting God's people with some specific threat or promise. In this context the basic metaphor of hearing functioned as linguistic corollary to the divine act of speaking.

4. *The prophet is a herald,* a broadcaster, whose vision and audition combined to convey an authoritative commission, expressed in actions visible and in words audible to a designated audience. The commission often fixed the boundaries for the authority: it extended to a particular audience for a particular period of time and covered a particular set of duties. The commission was invested with heavenly authority of which the prophet became the conduit. His personal sense of constraint, his awareness of a divine necessity, functioned to lay a similar constraint upon his audience: they must become aware of a similar necessity and must do whatever was commanded by the same authority. The obedience of the prophet was intended to elicit a similar obedience on the part of his audience.

5. *The prophet is an interpreter* of earlier messages, of Scripture. Because each prophetic disclosure of divine intention came in fulfillment of previous promises, the prophet's vocation included an interpretation of those promises as found in Scripture. To the extent that this vocation was unexpected and surprising, a reinterpretation of Scripture was called for. In this connection, meditation on particular passages in Scripture could precede, attend, or follow the vision and audition of the prophet. Such meditation, by conjoining current experiences and situations with the Law and the Prophets,

often produced radical revisions in the scriptural message to his constituency. Herein lay a perennial source of conflict between prophets and scribes.

6. *The prophet is an actor*, enacting his disclosure of the divine will. Just as the prophet was called to see the invisible heavenly counterpart of visible earthly events (or the visible earthly signs of invisible heavenly events) so, too he was often called to do powerful things within the view of his designated audience so that they might see these signs and, seeing, might come to comprehend their significance. These were often strange happenings which he did not himself cause, but which he was expected to interpret. Those signs might anticipate and provoke his message, or might accompany, follow, or reinforce it. In any case, they were integral to his vocation. They pointed beyond themselves to the mysterious and powerful presence of God, whose will for his people was hidden in those events until it should be revealed by the prophet. Prominent among such signs, as reported in Luke-Acts, were cures and exorcisms, together with the power to read the hearts of men. [10]

7. *The prophet is a community leader*, especially in the activity of worship. Just as the prophet had heard the inaudible voice of God, so he was called to make audible to God's people the message he had received. His vocation therefore became associated with preaching and teaching, with exhortation and consolation, with condemnation and assurance. In Luke's day certain conventional language forms had become typical of Christian prophets: beatitudes, woes, parables, oracular formulas. Prophets often led in the singing of communal songs of praise, using the tongues of men and angels, with rhetoric and rhythms appropriate to ecstatic joy and gratitude. Often, as we have noted, such songs would make explicit those reinterpretations of Scripture and those understandings of current events which the Spirit had disclosed. [11]

8. *The prophet is a catalyst*, whose power-laden deeds and words, combined with his unconventional relating of Scripture to current signs, tended to polarize his audience. His commission to speak was designed to make neutrality difficult if not impossible. Acceptance

or rejection were the two immediate options, and acute conflict between the two groups was thus produced. Luke saw conflict as inescapable between the successive generations of prophets and the successive generations of those who had persecuted them. Each true prophet shared in "the blood of all the prophets" (11:51). For Luke the chain of prophets was a chain of martyrs in the double sense: they were **witnesses** of the divine actions who became **victims** of deadly violence.[12]

9. *The prophet is an opponent of false prophets.* To Luke, as to most biblical writers, the polarization of the audience produced a polarization among the prophet-revealers themselves. Wherever the people recognized the strategic importance of prophecy and wherever one prophet appeared to provide divine guidance, there other prophets would challenge his reading of the divine mind. Not all could be true; some must be false. Yet all claimed and probably believed themselves to be authorized. Reference to the competing signs, to the interpretations of Scripture, and to visible credentials failed to settle the issue; each decision for one prophet was a decision against his competitors. The work of any true prophet effectively sharpened this dilemma on the part of his audience.

10. *The prophet is a tutor of other prophets.* When the assignment was to serve as God's messenger to the whole people for a substantial period of time as a fulfillment of covenant promises and with the prospect of martyrdom, the vocation frequently entailed the enlistment of a group of followers and disciples who would, by sharing the prophet's vocation, extend the scope of his work both in space and in time. With this group of colleagues he shared his gifts of understanding and power, and they inherited his mantle of social honor and hostility. The bond between master and disciples gave substantial weight to the master's *name*. Through this name they exercised his gifts of authority and power; by it his activity was extended through their actions. To it they gave witness, for it they suffered. To abandon their use of his name would be to cancel their commission.

I now take up for review Luke's understanding of the prophetic vocation of John, inasmuch as Jesus clearly saw his own mission as a continuation and consummation of John's work.

THE BAPTISM WHICH JOHN PREACHED

Luke traced the important beginnings of the Gospel to "the baptism which John preached," a baptism which embodied the authority of heaven. Moreover, this event had beeen much more than an episode in the experience of Jesus. John had succeeded in turning many of the sons of Israel to their God, preparing this people for the coming of their Lord (1:16–17).[13] Quite explicitly Luke identified the baptism of Jesus with the baptism of the whole community: "when all the people were baptized and when Jesus also had been baptized" (3:21). It was John's vocation to baptize both the people and the Messiah and to introduce them to each other by way of this common baptism. In the Lucan retrospect the Galileans who later gathered with Jesus in Jerusalem for the fateful Passover had first been drawn into the church by John's appeal. (Acts 1:21–22; 2:7) Even so, Luke's assertion that all the people had been baptized cannot do other than invite scepticism. All? Why should Luke have allowed such patent exaggerations to undermine his credibility? What about John's Pharisaic opponents, not to mention the political adversaries who killed him? The problem is only sharpened by noting that the term "people" (*laos*) connoted God's covenant people Israel. Did John actually baptize that entire community? Luke says yes, and in so doing exhibits a biblical and midrashic mode of thinking: the whole life of Israel can be condensed in a single event whenever the core and cohesion of the community is defined by that event. Consider the Midrash that says that *all* generations of Israel were present at Sinai and yet also says that the Torah *is* still given *wherever* a man receives it. Consider another midrash to the effect that on seeing the Red Sea devastation "all the nations of the world" renounced their idols; yet the same midrash announces that in the future the same nations would again renounce their idols.[14] The importance of an event is not measured by counting those present; rather is the reality of Israel, God's people, being defined by that event. Israel is here defined by repentance, by a coming out into the wilderness, by a turning toward the future, by the waiting for the coming of the one who would baptize Israel with Spirit and fire. Where men repent, there is Israel. In this exodus and in this eager hope Luke saw mirrored not only the birth of the church but the whole future of Israel. That future was partially fulfilled in the baptism of Jesus, for then the Spirit and fire descended on him. As Luke understood John's assignment, it was accomplished in a sense with his action in baptizing Jesus. With this deed John's commission as a prophet had been fully achieved, hence the premature reference in 3:20 to his imprisonment. John's promise would be further verified at Pentecost when the Spirit and fire would baptize "all flesh" (Acts 2:17).

Luke was obliged to recognize, however, that not all in Israel who had accepted John's baptism had also accepted the transfer of John's prophetic mantle to Jesus. The disciples of each prophet appear to have been confused by their relationship. Very early in his story, therefore, Luke took care to indicate Jesus' understanding of that link (5:33ff.; 7:18ff.) so that he might proceed with the training of his own school of prophets (8:1). Luke's first effort at clarifying the situation took the form of reporting the debate over fasting (5:33–39). Unlike Mark, he distinguished between the practice of John's disciples and that of the disciples of the Pharisees, concentrating on the significance of the praying and fasting of John's disciples. In two parables, the two garments and the two wineskins, Jesus warned men not to damage either the old or the new garments, either the new wine or the old wineskins. Although the new has its own distinctive function, the value of the old should not be denied. So disciples of both prophets should respect the divergent practices of both. Thus interpreted, these parables do not attack the old Law (the conventional interpretation). Rather they discourage the drawing of invidious comparisons between John and Jesus which would undercut the authority of John or the fasting which he had ordered. Jesus encouraged his followers to accept the roles of the two prophets as separate but complementary. Understood in this way, these parables embody virtually the same attitude as the twin parables of the children playing in the village square (7:32–35), in which John and Jesus are both viewed as children of wisdom whose call is obeyed by the same groups and refused by the same.

There is no doubt in Luke's mind that Jesus accepted John as an authentic spokesman of God. Nor is there doubt in our minds about Luke's view. In the birth stories John is identified as one who would come in the spirit and the power of Elijah (1:17). Professor Wink rightly says that Luke must himself be held responsible for that description.[15] Moreover, Luke introduced John's career with these words: "The word of God came to John . . . and he went into all the region about the Jordan, preaching a baptism of repentance for the forgiveness of sins" (3:2–3). There are several noteworthy items here. "The word of God came": this is a conventional way of introducing a prophet's utterance, in which God first speaks to the prophet who in turn speaks to God's people. "In the wilderness": this phrase presents John's manner of life as a fulfillment of Isaiah's prophecy (vv. 2, 4). "All flesh shall see the salvation of God" (v. 6): in these words Luke expressed the conviction that God desired to reach through John a widening circle of auditors (the multitudes, Israel, all flesh). "A baptism of repentance": this action of John and the people is assumed to be an authentic response to God's demand. "For the forgiveness of sins": Luke here identified this forgiveness with the gift of God's salvation (v. 6). No less sweeping and no less authoritative were John's warnings against the judgment to come, a judgment which made obsolete all traditional reliance on father Abraham, and which threatened all who failed to treat themselves as vulnerable to the winnowing fan (vv. 10–14). Preaching, exhorting, warning, baptizing, crying, predicting doom and dawn—the whole of John's work was interpreted by Luke as the word of God exploding in the ears of his people. In John, Elijah's work, Isaiah's word, and Malachi's prediction were being fulfilled (vv. 15–17).

Just as Luke took seriously John's testimony about Jesus, so he took with equal seriousness Jesus' testimony about John. Just as the fetus John leaped in recognition of Mary's baby, so, too, Mary's trip to Elizabeth constituted prophetic recognition of Elizabeth's baby. Karl Barth rightly made much of the famous Isenheim altarpiece, in which attention is focused on the finger of John pointing toward Jesus. Theologians usually ignore the equally dramatic scene in Luke 7:24–27 in which Jesus' finger points toward John.

We have noted that the ultimate audience assigned to John was the same as that assigned to Jesus: God's covenant people and, through them, "all flesh." We should also note a similar convergence in the more immediate audiences, the crowds (*ochloi*) which, as representatives of Israel, came flocking to the Jordan.[16] The austere prophet saw their exodus as a flight from the coming wrath of God. Jesus and Luke saw it also as a true perception of John's heavenly authority which induced mass repentance, baptism, and a readiness to obey the other crisis demands of God (20:1–8). From all directions a diverse lot had come, including soldiers, customs collectors, and harlots; they served as symbols of compromise and complicity, so that their arrival at the Jordan became a sign of God's ability to turn stones into sons. Their baptism was the index of their total dependence on God's demand and promise as mediated by John. It was in these humbled multitudes, a *laos* in the moment of renewal, that Luke located the beginnings of the church. Jesus appeared among them and was baptized with them. From them he drew his own band of disciples. The same crowds, representing the same *laos*, remained the primary audience for both prophets and even continued to be the visitors whom Paul welcomed in the final episode in the Book of Acts (28:30).

John and Jesus attracted the same groups in great numbers; they also repelled the same groups. Jesus was not the first to polarize the nation; he simply continued the process begun by John. The same Herod, according to Luke, was implicated in the execution of both. Nor can one detect any distinction in the hostility exerted toward these prophets by elders, priests, scribes, Pharisees, the "rulers" of the *laos*. The more enthusiasm among the despised groups, the more animosity among the respectable. The more violently the establishment reacted, the more hypnotized were the crowds. Lash and backlash operated to make inescapable the query "Who is this?" (3:15). It is significant that Luke's Jesus took the initiative in answering that query; even more significant that he answered by an appeal to the action of the crowds who had first rushed out to the wilderness to hear John, but who had later gone with Jesus from city to city (7:11, 16, 24). The very crowds who now hailed Jesus as a great prophet (7:16) were forced to hear his testimony concerning John as a prophet and even as a *super*prophet (7:26).

Luke, using the Q traditions, makes clear how Jesus taught his own followers about the important role of John. If they had begun to accept Jesus' authority as a great prophet (7:16), they must now, on his authority, recognize John as a great prophet, indeed as "something more than a prophet" (7:26). Through the Scriptures God himself had declared the interdependence of the two prophets (7:27); accordingly men could not hail Jesus as emissary of God without simultaneously accepting John as such. John's wilderness regimen, his fasting, his repudiation of luxury, his inflexible loyalty to "the word of God," his scorn of kings and lawyers, had been valid signs of his vocation as messenger from God. The contrast between John's weeping and Jesus' dancing (7:32) had *nothing* to do with the validity of either. Luke saw Jesus' words as ruling out any temptation among his followers to despise the man through whom God had prepared the way for Jesus: "Among those born of women none is greater than John" (7:28). (Later we will discuss the second half of this verse. Although it adds an important qualification, that addition by no means cancels the legitimacy of this first tribute.) The same children who justified the divine wisdom that spoke in one prophet should justify the divine wisdom that speaks in the other.

There is no doubt that Luke viewed John as a prophet *like Elijah*. It may be true that Luke made less of Elijah as a prototype for John than did the other synoptists, as Walter Wink argues.[17] Even so, Luke continued to view the similarities as providing significant clues to John's vocation. His greatness was comparable to Elijah's, since he came in the same spirit and power. Both were prophets of the Most High, sent to convey knowledge of salvation to God's people, to bring that people to a state of emergency, to repentance, and to renewed covenantal fidelities. In both, the promises to the fathers had reached fulfillment. The birth stories of John celebrated the realization of the prophecies of Malachi (2:1–4:3) which quite explicitly announced the return of Elijah "before the great and terrible day of the Lord" (4:5). This implied quite certainly the conviction that the work of John as eschatological prophet marked the inauguration of God's judgment on his people. Elijah, whose assumption into heaven had made him continually accessible to Israel and whose return from heaven would mark strategic action on God's part, had released his spirit and power on this wilderness prophet whose ascetic calling of Israel to the Jordan linked their act of baptism to no less than three pivotal disclosures in earlier history: to Elijah, to Isaiah, and to Malachi.

JOHN AND THE VOCATION OF JESUS

Luke, then, saw both John and Jesus as true prophets with authority and assignment from God. The major differences were due to their different assignments. The more final and decisive the assignment given to Jesus, the more strategic the work of the one who prepared his way, and vice versa. Both had been sent by God as fulfillment of promises issued to his people through Isaiah (3:4–6; 4:18f.). Both could have said with reference to those promises: "Today this Scripture has been fulfilled." Both recognized that that fulfillment had produced a reinterpretation of that Scripture and this plunged them into bitter altercation with the authorized exegetes. They joined in giving that double witness to God's judgment which the Law itself required. Both accepted the baptism of repentance as the God-ordained beginning of the new order, and both viewed the rejection of that baptism as excluding the Pharisees and lawyers from the purposes of God (7:30). The work of both men precipitated the same urgent question: "Who is this?" Answers to that question produced a cleavage between Israel as represented by the crowds and by their rulers. The line of cleavage followed a boundary drawn by three inseparable actions: obedience to these two prophets as spokesmen of God's judgment and redemption, acceptance of their interpretation of Scripture in the light of contemporary signs of God's presence, and participation in baptism as the sacrament of the end-time in which final future judgment had been made operative "today."

Certainly Luke did not encourage his readers to promote Jesus by demoting John. To him the association of the two prophets did not demean either. His report that the crowds viewed Jesus as continuing the work of John was not designed to call attention to a major mistake (9:7, 19); rather, such a view marked a step toward understanding the divine mission of *both* prophets. Let me, then, draw up a summary of common elements in that mission. First, we observe that the vocations of both John and Jesus were interpreted as continuing common traditions and as analogous to the same prototypes. It is clear that Luke collated the story of John and the tradition of Elijah (1:16f.; 1:76f.).[18] There are almost as impressive parallels between Jesus and the same prophet (4:25; 7:11–17; 9:54; 12:54–56; 24:49; Acts 1:9).[19] In certain respects the relation of John to Jesus echoes the relation of Elijah to Elisha.[20] The work of both prophets is explicitly described as a fulfillment of the prophecies of Isaiah (Lk. 3:4–6; 4:18f.) and Malachi (Lk. 1:17, 76; 7:27). It is also likely that Luke believed that both gave similar reinterpretations of the Law, with similar appraisals of the current renewals of the wilderness wanderings and the Abrahamic covenant. Like that of Elijah and Elisha (4:25–27), the openness of Jesus to Gentile needs is entirely comparable to John's attitude toward the children of Abraham whom God could and did raise up from stones (3:8). The requirement that Jews must undergo a baptism usually required of proselytes implied "that the whole nation was apostate and sinful and if it was to become the people of God it must enter the society of God's people through repentance and baptism."[21]

Second, we observe similar accents in their commission under the same God. They exerted the same authority in response to a heavenly call which conveyed the command to preach the Word of the Lord, to witness, to exhort. They were impelled by similar degrees of

urgency, for they announced "the imminent intervention of God and
not an intervention after thirty or forty years."[22] This prospect was
seen by both to augur a great threat and a great promise. The two
were inseparable; as men fled from the coming wrath they sought the
coming redemption. "There are profound reasons for this: grace and
judgment belong together."[23] They relayed this message to the same
audiences; very likely their disciples were drawn from the same circles. And they summoned their hearers to immediate, unqualified,
self-denying obedience. Repentance was viewed by both as marking
decisive preparation for the new age, as in fact identifying the boundary between old and new. For both, this repentance was an act of
total *kenosis* whereby individuals representing the whole *laos* accepted the position of extreme poverty and humility in which, as
devoid of power and rights and merits before God as were the Gentiles, they relied wholly on God's gift of a new future. The good
time ahead would come only for those who had readied themselves
by such *kenosis*. What T. W. Manson said, in the Shaffer Lectures of
1939, about John's prophetic call applies equally to Jesus:

> He found himself caught up irresistibly by the mighty current of the
> divine authority in human affairs, appointed to tasks which he dared not
> refuse, furnished with a message which he must at all costs deliver.[24]

Both reinterpreted the past and offered future options in a way to
provide new horizons for present decisions. That future horizon embraced the expectation of a coming baptism with Spirit and fire, of a
gift, through that baptism, of forgiveness and release from captivity,
and of a fulfillment of God's covenants with Israel.

Even when judged in terms of external criteria their contemporaries recognized their kinship. They were alike in repudiating the
claims of wealth, security, political power, and the slightest desire
for "the essentials" of family life, not to mention the luxuries. They
knew what wilderness existence required and were not inexperienced
in the disciplines of fasting. Prayer was more than a conventional
practice and had become a means of daily survival. They aroused
turbulent excitement, often dangerous, among the same groups,

mostly the ostracized, alienated, or powerless. They encountered the hatreds and suspicions of those who had a stake in the economic and political struggles, whether as rebels or as professionals. Moreover, there is evidence that each recognized kinship in the vocation of the other. In the end, of course, both suffered death as a direct consequence of their prophetic vocation.

It is this kinship in prophetic vocation that the birth stories, with their unique kind of witness, so deftly articulate. The mothers are kinfolk, and each recognizes the prenatal call of the other. The same angel conveyed similar messages to the parents of both; in fact, the Holy Spirit enabled the parents to prophesy along with the other actors in the drama, for example, the shepherds, Simeon, Anna. At the birth of both infants scriptural promises are fulfilled, promises covering events which would happen even after the deaths of both. The stories give their own acknowledgement of divergence between their later assignments, but the divergence itself corroborates the divine correlation. God guides the development of each child toward "the day of manifestation to Israel" (1:80; 2:52). There is ominous recognition of the passion of each, but no suggestion that such a prospect represents anything but a majestic, if also mysterious, consummation of heaven's designs. The birth of both infants is a miraculous sign of God's omnipotence in the context of man's impotence, of God's power to use the wrath of men to praise him.[25]

Let this summary suffice for demonstrating Luke's conviction of the kinship between Jesus' vocation and John's. His conviction is a challenge to us, in these latter days, to discern in the prophetic message and mission of John substantial clues to the character of Jesus' vocation. At the minimum, our conclusion must be this: the greater the distance between our own attitudes toward Jesus and toward John the Baptist, the more we have ignored the Christian testimony of Luke. It was through John that Jesus was linked to "the goodly fellowship of the prophets." It was through John that God made ready a people prepared for the Lord (1:17). If John was a failure and his story a tragedy, as T.W.Manson quite wrongly says,[26] so was Jesus'. If Jesus' vocation resulted in the vindication of God's pledge to his people, John also participated in that victory. It was in fulfillment of John's prophecy that at Pentecost the whole company of Jesus' disciples were baptized by fire and the Spirit, and that God fulfilled Moses' prayer that all of his people should become prophets (Num. 11:29). Luke viewed the gift of prophecy as binding every Christian to John, fusing them together into the same vocation.[27]

Do ministers today sense any kinship with John as sharing the same vocation? The honest answer is, I think, a blunt no. The threads of affection and loyalty to him are tenuous indeed. Nothing in our hearts resonates to Jesus' tribute to John as the greatest among men. Our ministry has nothing to do with his, nor his with ours. Since this is true, it is no wonder that we have neglected to use the charismatic ministry of John as providing major clues to the vocation of Jesus, no wonder that our christologies are so detached from this original context.

This situation prompts the question: on what terms can we reenter Luke's world in which the work of John was understood to introduce and to inform not only the vocation of Jesus but that of every Christian? This question is probably more important than any I have raised up to this point; yet I cannot do more than to indicate the bare framework of an answer. Any reentry into Luke's world presupposes and requires a world view the opposite of the "flat-earthers," those radical secularists whose earth is limited to one dimension; it requires a world view which gives absolute primacy to the reality of God and his governance of man's affairs. Moreover, we will never reenter the world of the prophets unless we concede that God actually has available various means of communication with his people, means which explode the firmness and fixity of those patterns of thought by which we have domesticated the anarchies of history, making ourselves slaves of immanence in the process. An understanding of any prophet requires that we become aware of the power of the Spirit to bring us to a repentance before God that is radical enough to include an abandonment of all illusions of competence—intellectual, moral, professional—and a new openness to recognize in our own hearts the signs of renewed battles between God and Satan, struggles in which again there is ample room for flights of angels and demons. It is not necessary that each of us should repeat the vocation of John, but his trumpet call forces us to join either the *laos* which was baptized or the religious and political rulers who rejected his authority. We should not ignore the possibility that the charismatic phenomena which are now so active in various quarters, whatever their deficiencies when compared with biblical precedents, may help us to reenter a world where God is offering fresh guidance to his people, who well know what it is to live in the wilderness while waiting for a prophet like Elijah.

Such an answer to an important question is all too sketchy, but a fuller answer may be forthcoming in our final chapter.

5

*The expected prophet, the second Moses and second
Savior of his people, is persecuted as a small child by
a wicked king, is again called by God out of Egypt,
gathers his people in the wilderness, proclaims from
the mountain the law of a new covenant, repeats the
miraculous feedings which belonged to Israel's
primeval period during the first journey through the
wilderness, and recapitulates and surpasses the
miraculous signs of the ancient prophets Elijah and
Elisha.* [1]

JESUS AS A PROPHET
LIKE MOSES

IT IS SIGNIFICANT, to a greater degree
than is often recognized, that all four Gospels speak of Jesus as a
prophet. Certainly in Luke this term is used without reservation to
refer to Jesus' vocation. Jesus' disciples thought of him as a prophet
"mighty in deed and word" (24:19). Crowds responded to some of
his mighty deeds with the accolade "a great prophet has arisen
among us" (7:16). When enemies demanded more convincing signs,
their very demand presupposed that Jesus had asserted claims to authority which they had rejected. On occasion they argued: if this
man were a prophet, he would have known or have done something
far more convincing (7:39). At the trial brutal soldiers ridiculed
such a claim by blindfolding him, beating him, and then asking,
"Who struck you?" It was as a false prophet and king that Jesus was

arrested, tried, arrayed in royal robes, and condemned to death. More to the point, Jesus clearly associated himself with the long chain of prophets (4:24; 13:33). Nowhere is this more obvious than in the opening visit to Nazareth when he declared that the Spirit of the Lord had descended upon him. He thus identified himself both with the mission of Isaiah and with the messenger whom Isaiah had foretold. In announcing the inauguration of the day of redemption, he explicitly compared his vocation to that of Elijah and Elisha, and he interpreted his rejection in Nazareth as a vindication of that connection. We should not easily or quickly despise this self-designation.

That, however, is precisely what many modern theologians and preachers do, supposing that this christological category is less impressive than others. What is so remarkable or unique about the claim that Jesus was a prophet? Such a claim seems to say no more than do many Muslims and Jews in giving their mild tribute to the prophet Jesus. Oscar Cullmann, for instance, treats the prophetic role as an "ordinary human professional category" which, because it lacks a recognition of Jesus' uniqueness, makes it irrelevant to the solution of "the christological problem." To be sure, Cullmann recognizes, in a halfhearted way, a distinction between speaking of Jesus as *a* prophet and as *the* prophet; but even the latter image is quickly dismissed as "too narrow to do justice to the early Christian faith," since it applies only to Jesus' earthly work as a preacher of repentance and fails to include his "conscious vicarious suffering and dying," his continuing redemptive work as the exalted Christ, and the completion of that work in the parousia.[2]

On this issue I oppose Cullmann and support John Knox, who in his Shaffer Lectures denied that the prophetic vocation precluded uniqueness. "Every true prophet," he writes, "is aware of a unique calling. The word of God has come to him—to him uniquely, and, in a sense, alone." Knox also insisted that we go astray when we set limits to the importance of this vocation. "No one can say how high and deep it may be. . . . Nor can any arbitrary boundary be set to the depth of any particular prophet's sense of vocation or to the greatness of the work he believes God has given him to do."[3] The highest appraisal of Jesus' work as redeemer and revealer of the Most High God does not exclude his possession of this charismatic gift.

Even so, we must admit that there are vast contrasts in the significance of the work of various prophets. Consider, for example, Simeon, Agabus, Silas, the daughters of Philip, and the disciples in Ephesus. The wider the range of this charismatic gift, the more necessary it is to discriminate among its recipients. How may one prophetic calling be distinguished from others?

The first answer can be advanced in theoretical terms:

How large is the audience to whom God sends a particular spokesman: one man, a small assembly, the whole of Israel, all men?

How long a tenure is given: one day or journey, a limited period, a lifetime, the agelong mission of God's people?

How much is at stake in the existing crisis, and how strategic are the decisions which God requires of the prophet's audience?

How radically is God revising his earlier covenants and forming new covenants which replace the old?

With what earlier prophets is the vocation of the contemporary prophet to be compared?

Luke's portrait of Jesus as a prophet gives clear answers to these questions. Jesus was explicitly commissioned as a messenger to the whole of Israel, a mission which ultimately included "all the nations." The indications of the time-span were equally inclusive: until the day of the Lord (Acts 2:20), until his return from heaven (Acts 1:11), or until all his enemies had been subjugated (Acts 2:35). Responses to his intervention were absolutely decisive, in that they determined the fate of men, cities, and nations in the final judgment (2:37–40). He offered a covenant to Israel which fulfilled the earlier covenant with Abraham (3:25) and defined the boundaries of the house of Israel (3:23). In comparing his vocation to that of predecessors, Luke chose as analogues pivotal figures from the past and used each analogy to indicate the greater significance of Jesus. The vocation of Jesus is seen as a fulfillment of "*all* the prophets"; more specifically, Luke links his work to many earlier spokesmen: Abel, Noah, Abraham, Lot, Samuel, David, Solomon, Elijah, Elisha, Isaiah, Jonah, Joel, Zechariah. Each of these links carries a strategic force. However, in Luke's mind the most strategic among them is the link to Moses. This link is explicitly accented in two key sermons in the Book of Acts, those of Peter and of Stephen. Let us listen first to Peter's address in Solomon's Porch:

> "What God foretold by the mouth of all the prophets, that his Christ should suffer, he thus fulfilled. Repent, therefore, and turn again, that your sins may be blotted out, that times of refreshing may come from the presence of the Lord, and that he may send the Christ appointed for you, Jesus, whom heaven must receive until the time for establishing all that God spoke by the mouth of his holy prophets from of old. Moses said, 'The Lord God will raise up for you *a prophet from your brethren as he raised me up*. You shall listen to him in whatever he tells you. And it shall be that every soul that does not listen to that prophet shall be destroyed from the people' " (Deut. 18:15–16 in Acts 3:18–23).

Operating in Luke's appeal to this text we observe several basic convictions:

Moses is considered to be more a prophet than a lawgiver; his work linked him to all the other prophets, and especially to Abraham and to Samuel.

Jesus' whole ministry is described as that of a prophet raised up as Moses had been.

It is assumed to be important that this Messiah should have been raised up "from among your brethren" and "for you."

The fulfillment of all the earlier prophets including Moses is explicitly related to the suffering of God's Messiah.

The obligation to hear and to obey this prophet is as binding as the same obligation vis-à-vis Moses. In fact, it is more binding, inasmuch as it is Moses who here commands the men of Israel to obey this Messiah, reminiscent of the heavenly command at the Transfiguration.

As in the case of Moses, any refusal to listen to this Messiah would spell "destruction from the people."

The obligation to obey this prophet, this appointed Messiah, is oriented toward the activity of repentance and forgiveness, present anticipations of the times of refreshing from the presence of the Lord.

The fulfillment of the promise to Moses entails the fulfillment of an earlier covenant with Abraham, a promise of blessing extended to "all the families of earth" (3:25).

The use of the category *prophet* to describe Jesus' role coalesces with other categories without any sense of incompatibility: God's servant, the Holy and Righteous One, the author of life, God's Messiah.

The phrase *to raise up a prophet* has a surprisingly broad definition, for it covers the total assignment given to Jesus. The thought does not focus on the eschatological preaching of Jesus before Calvary; rather, the same verb is used to denote both Moses' raising and Jesus' resurrection (3:22, 26). Even that event must be viewed broadly in such a way as to include the messianic sufferings, the blotting out of sins, the arrival of times of refreshing, and the final establishment of the promise given to Abraham. In appealing to the raising up of this prophet, Luke had in mind primarily the postresurrection activity of this Messiah in Israel.

These observations concerning Peter's sermon demonstrate the importance in Luke's mind of this typological metaphor: Abraham, Moses, and Jesus are three prophets without whom Israel would lose its identity, its mission, its destiny. Without them "all the families of the earth" would be without hope. In short, given the context of this sermon, no christological confession could be more decisive or more exalted than this: a prophet like Moses.

Just as the sermon of Peter illuminated the story of Jesus by reference to Moses, the sermon of Stephen illuminated the story of Moses by reference to Jesus (Acts 7:35–43). If we did not know in advance its location, we might apply the following verse to either prophet: "He supposed that his brethren understood that God was giving them deliverance by his hand, but they did not understand" (7:25). Like Jesus, Moses had been made a judge and ruler over God's people (v. 35); like Jesus, Moses had been anointed prophet by vision and audition, had received "living oracles," had been empowered to give signs and wonders. By the hand of the angel he had been guided in daring and patient leadership first in Egypt, then at the Red Sea, and during the wilderness wanderings. So firmly in Christian traditions had the Mosaic analogy become established that we may discern in Stephen's speech how the image of Jesus began to shape the image of Moses, not least in accenting the significance of rejection and suffering on the part of this predecessor of Jesus.

To understand the full force of the Mosaic typology we need to recover the role of Moses in the synagogue traditions of Luke's own day. To prove that a particular stereotype was current at a specific time and place is not easy. That Luke would have known the scriptural stories about Moses is, of course, certain. With less certainty but with a high degree of probability we can affirm as available to Luke the image of Moses in such documents as the Wisdom of Solomon, the Assumption of Moses, and some of the Qumran writings. More problematic, yet still significant, are Mosaic traditions handed down among the rabbis and in the Samaritan literature. The best recent survey of all these traditions has been provided by Wayne Meeks, from whose summary I have selected seven specific features:[4]

1. The term *prophet* "was one of the most frequent designations of Moses around the turn of the eras." Within the entire sequence of messengers from God he is mentioned variously as the first prophet, the source of prophecy, and as the teacher of all the other prophets.

2. Moses' prophetic career had centered in his ascent to Sinai to receive living oracles; this ascent had been "widely regarded as an ascent to heaven." There he had received the Torah and had learned secrets and mysteries of vital import to the destiny of Israel. He had been enthroned, crowned, robed in light, endowed with the Name and with power to speak for God. "Whatever he uttered, it seemed that one heard God himself speaking."

3. Coming to earth, that is, on his descent from Sinai, he came as

God's *apostolos* and was rejected by Israel, this being tantamount to Israel's rejection of God. Moses' prophecies were linked to his rejection and sufferings. As a true prophet he showed his willingness to die for Israel. In some sense this death was vicarious.

4. Moses' prophetic role tended to coalesce with other roles— lawgiver, shepherd, king, priest, advocate, servant. Typological thought tended to fuse these various images rather than to separate them. Some of these titles may have entered the Christian traditions by way of the Mosaic saga.

5. Moses was a prophet who redeemed his people by rescuing them from captivity, from the Red Sea, from the wilderness. This saving work had embraced also his intercession in heaven for Israel; in heaven God had hidden Moses for the life of the age to come. As redeemer his work had become a prototype of coming deliverance: "As the first redeemer was, so shall the latter redeemer be" (R. Berekiah).

6. This redemptive work had been signalled by signs and wonders, for example, the feeding of Israel in the wilderness, where Moses served as a shepherd of his people.

7. All later prophets maintained a direct link to Moses. "Every prophet who arose repeated the prophecy of his predecessor in order to clarify his prophecy." "His prophecy was like the surrounding sea, for from it seventy prophets had prophesied without any diminishing of it" (Momar Marqah, ii, 12). Since Moses had been given the secrets of the ends of the ages, all later prophets remained in a sense dependent on him.

Such a summary is hazardous because it brings together features which may well have been current in different places and different periods. Even so, these traditions demonstrate the potential significance of the Mosaic typology in Luke's thought. When Luke asserted that God had fulfilled his promise to Moses by raising up a prophet like him, he tapped a huge reservoir of latent images, expressive of Israel's strongest memories and most vital hopes. Virtually all the images of divine deliverance that had been embodied in stories of the Exodus from captivity in Egypt to the Promised Land became applicable to God's action in raising Jesus.

One thing is now certain: in Luke's day a lively expectation of the coming of a prophet like Moses existed in many different circles. Among the Samaritans, in the Essene community at Qumran, and among the rabbis, the presence of such an expectation cannot be denied. Nor can we doubt the fact that this expectation was based firmly on the Law, not only the promise found in Deuteronomy 18:15–18 but also on the description of the Exodus wanderings of Israel as prototype of later deliverances. Moreover, it is entirely probable that II Isaiah had extensively developed this analogy and that this development was continued in the New Testament. The portrait of the Servant in Isaiah 40 and following was partially based on the similar designation of Moses as wise, faithful, and meek; more surely the descriptions of salvation in II Isaiah are saturated with the memories of deliverance from Egypt to the Promised Land; and it is certain that Luke frequently turned to II Isaiah for capsule summaries of the vocation of both John and Jesus. The portraits in Luke's gallery of Jesus as prophet, revealer, teacher, servant, judge, ruler, Son of God, covenant-maker, deliverer, have too many points of contact with the portrait of Moses to be accidental. To comprehend those points fully we need, of course, to project ourselves into the midst of a community in which the emotional thrust of memories and hopes was provided in large part by reverence and gratitude for the work of Moses. For Luke, no analogy to the redemptive work of Jesus could be more evocative or more far-reaching than this comparison to Moses.

We should specially note the presence in the mission of the two prophets of rejection and suffering. This is a dominant motif of the two sermons in Acts (3:13–15, 17–23; 7:23–27, 35, 39–41). For both Moses and Jesus, rejection was the prime constituent in the suffering—love for the people being frustrated by their blindness. Their rejection of proffered deliverance was tantamount to crucifixion.[5] The rejection of the prophets was nothing less than resistance to the Holy Spirit (7:51) and disobedience to "the law as delivered by angels" (7:53). In both cases salvation was conceived as deliverance from captivity; in both it was repudiated because the demands of God were excessive, the sacrifices too arduous, the promises too distant and intangible. In both, the rejection by the people and the punishment by God were seen to be perennial and permanent.[6] Luke sees death as the sign under which all prophets stand, their solidarity being matched by the solidarity of all generations of persecutors (7:51–52). It is entirely likely, therefore, that the traditional image of Moses was one of the factors contributing to the early Christian conviction that the Son of man must suffer, with his followers, in the fulfillment of prophecy (Lk. 12:49–51; 13:31–35; 18:31–34).[7]

When we read the Gospel against this background, many of Jesus' actions gain in significance. For instance, his readiness to set aside the Law after a mountain retreat (5:17–26) can more readily be understood as the dramatic gesture of a prophet like Moses; his appointment of the Twelve (6:12–16), his dispatch of the seventy "prophets and kings" (10:1 ff.), and his covenant with the twelve "rulers" at the Passover can be seen as establishing continuity with Israel's past without diminishing their radical novelty. Nor should we overlook the subtle effect of this typology on Jesus' teachings. We have seen how the prophetic vocation normally embraced the work of admonition and exhortation, with a distinctive range of oral forms, and how that vocation presupposed the association of the prophets' teaching with the authorization of God. That being true, how much more true in the case of a prophet like Moses in a community in which the highest reverence had been accorded that prototype.

One of the passages in Luke's Gospel most clearly influenced was the familiar transfiguration story, where we hear multiple echoes from the Mosaic saga, especially from Exodus 24. This narrative appears immediately following two episodes in which first Herod and then the crowds appraise Jesus by comparing him to John, to Elijah, and to "one of the old prophets." In the preceding context Luke also locates the story of Jesus, like Moses, feeding the multitude in the wilderness. Still more noteworthy is the fact that when the trans-figured Lord talked with the glorified Moses and Elijah, they dis-cussed his *exodus*. Finally, it is significant that the command issued in Luke 9:35 was the same as that in Deuteronomy 18:15 and in Acts 3:22: "Listen to him." Moreover, when we seek in the Lucan context for the precise content of the mandate to which they must listen, the nearest and most likely answer is provided by the saying "the Son of man must suffer" (9:22, 44). All this expands the scope of Luke's understanding of what it meant for God to raise up Jesus as he raised up Moses. Jesus' prophetic vocation included his suffering (the core of both Acts sermons), his rejection by Israel, his exodus, his glori-fication, his continued power to gather the scattered tribes, to feed them, and to heal the sick.

C.F. Evans has developed an extensive set of parallels between the Lucan account of Jesus and the Deuteronomic account of Moses. Most significant perhaps are the coincidences between Jesus' journey to Jerusalem and that of Moses to the Promised Land, the sending of the twelve apostles/spies to represent the twelve tribes, and the ap-pointment of the seventy missionaries/elders to share in the prophets' work. Evans concludes his survey with the following words:

> The conclusion is difficult to resist that the evangelist has selected and arranged his material in such a way as to present it in a Deuteronomic sequence. His motive for doing so is not far to seek; it will have sprung from the conviction . . . that Jesus was the prophet like unto Moses.[8]

Nor should we overlook the significance of Pentecost in the Mosaic saga, the annual celebration of the giving of the Law through Moses to God's people, as the setting chosen for the descent of the Spirit on the Twelve and on the 120. But more on that later.[9]

CONTRASTS BETWEEN JOHN AND JESUS

Having examined the Mosaic connections, let us now look again at John the Baptist. In the preceding chapter we examined the features in which the vocations of these two prophets were comparable. So extensive were these features that we can readily understand why John was mentioned first whenever popular appraisals of Jesus were reported (Lk. 9:7–9, 18–22). Members of the crowd and even Herod surmised that Jesus might be John "all over again," to use T.W. Manson's phrase. We must now devote attention to the features of Jesus' vocation which were unlike John's, observing, however, that in Luke's mind even these contrasts represent the fulfillment of God's promises to John. Some of those features appear immediately in Luke's accounts of John's prophecy and of Jesus' own baptism.

Luke's account of John's message specifies three respects in which Jesus' work would differ:

1. John's successor would be mightier and worthier.
2. He would baptize the people with the Holy Spirit.
3. He would baptize them with the unquenchable fires of God's final harvest.

Part of the promise is fulfilled almost immediately: Jesus is baptized with the Holy Spirit (3:22). Moreover, this baptism remained effective through all the following episodes in which Jesus was "full of the Holy Spirit," "led by the Spirit," "returned in the power of the Spirit." These third-person comments reach a climax with Jesus' first-person announcement: "The Spirit of the Lord is upon me" (4:1, 14, 18).

At a later point in his story Luke would distinguish the two epochs in a summary: "The law and the prophets were until John; since then the good news of the kingdom of God is preached" (16:16). We will adopt that formula as a way of focusing many of the distinguishing features of Jesus' vocation: *until John, the baptism with water; since John, the baptism with the Spirit.*

What that baptism meant for the prophetic vocation of Jesus himself is described in multiple fashion by Luke. It meant the opening of heaven, with the attendant vision, audition, election, and commission (3:22). It meant a struggle in the wilderness with the devil, with the attendant decisions concerning how Jesus would deal with such issues as authority, worship, security, and freedom. "I beheld Satan fall like lightning from heaven." The intensity of temptation and of the conflict with evil made Jesus' victory an indication of how he had become mightier than John through the Spirit-baptism. It meant that Jesus could now proclaim with authority the fulfillment of Isaiah's prophecy in his own work, each item as recounted in the Nazareth sermon marking an advance over John (for example, the release of captives and the healing of the blind). In fulfilling John's prophecy, this particular baptism with the Spirit simultaneously fulfilled Isaiah's promise and inaugurated the proclamation of good news to the poor. Finally, the baptism of the Spirit assisted Jesus in determining who would be his major audience. Baptized along with "all the people" (*laos*, 3:21), he was assigned a special responsibility for the poor, the captives, the blind, and the oppressed (4:18), for all those who because of economic, political, and religious helplessness had all their hopes invested in "the acceptable year of the Lord."

Jesus found this particular audience not in Nazareth but in Capernaum. There the Spirit-propelled good news to the poor took the form of releasing men from demons and from debilitating fevers (4:31–41). These anecdotes justify the following epitome: *until John, men were captive to demons and sickness; since John, they have been freed.* In these stories we discern the effects of the victories which the Spirit had enabled Jesus to win in the wilderness. In him the demons had met their match; God had given Jesus more authority over them than he had given John. In line with John's promise, the demons had recognized the coming of a mightier and holier one, sent to destroy them (4:34) and to release their captives (4:18c). Victory over them constituted a major reason why this preaching of the kingdom represented good news as yet unknown to John (Lk. 7:21–23; 16:16; Acts 2:22). Luke indicated a further distinction between John and his successor in describing the first encounter between Jesus and the Pharisees (5:17–26), where "the power of the Lord was with him to heal." That phrase, "the power of the Lord," identifies this healing as an earthly sign of the heavenly power conferred on him in his anointing as prophet. In this case the prophet wrought the cure simply by his declaration, "Man, your sins are forgiven." The reaction of the Pharisees was immediate: "Blasphemy!" Since only God can forgive sins, any man who claims to do so commits blasphemy (a logic and a sin which have become unintelligible in these latter sophisticated days). The logic was right but the inference wrong. It is true to say that only God can forgive sins, but wrong to accuse Jesus of blasphemy, because God has given that authority to the Son of man on earth. *Until John, the baptism of repentance for the forgiveness of sins; since John, Jesus' baptism by the Spirit enabled him to forgive sins.*

We have skipped over one episode in the Lucan story of beginnings which must now be mentioned: the archetypal call of the four fishermen, in 5:1–11. Jesus' assignment as a prophet included the enlistment and direction of those who were to fish for men. In their experience of failure apart from his presence, and of success when they obeyed him, they discovered both their own sinfulness and their future dependence on him. Although John, too, had called disciples, Luke detected in Jesus' call a power and an authority as distinctive as that of Moses. To convey this difference, Luke has transformed a Marcan account which was nonmiraculous into a miraculous fish-catching event. This change was probably suggested by Jesus' promise to the four fishermen (Mk. 1:17). To Luke that promise became nothing less than "a symbolic anticipation of the whole vocation at the time of the call,"[10] not unlike Paul's confession that he had been set aside from his mother's womb, (Gal. 1:15), nor unlike the prenatal calls of John and Jesus (Lk. 1; 2). *Until John, disciples shared in the baptism of repentance; since John, disciples were enlisted in a vocation of fishing.*

One reason for Jesus' own effectiveness in fishing appears to have been his attitude toward sinners. As the call of Levi indicated (5:27–32), Jesus took the initiative in enlisting followers from the despised and alienated groups of society. John had urged them to come out to the wilderness; Jesus sought them out in the cities.

More than this, Jesus insisted on eating and drinking with them; this action was a form of adopting them into his family and of sealing a firm covenant with them. God had chosen as heirs of his realm the riffraff, the ne'er-do-wells, the cultural misfits. By recognizing this choice of such persons to celebrate the dawn of a new age, Jesus proclaimed their genuine liberation "today." The actuality of that liberation was measured both by the grateful surprise of the sinners and by the angry chagrin of the righteous. Luke makes subtle use, for instance, of the story of Jesus' anointing by a woman in a Pharisee's house (7:36–50). Jesus' host said *to himself,* "If this man were a prophet, he would have known that this woman is a sinner." A true prophet would have discerned the secrets of the woman's heart, and seeing, would have shunned her. Luke shows how Jesus reversed that logic. That he was a prophet is beyond doubt, for he not only knew all about the woman, but he could read even the unspoken thoughts of his host. It was indeed *as* a true prophet that he had relayed God's forgiveness to the woman, a forgiveness adequate to cover the greatest sin. It was as a prophet that he could dismiss the woman as saved and in peace. *Until John, the summons to repentance; since John, unconditional fellowship with forgiven sinners.* John had called for sinners to flee the coming wrath; Jesus saw the kingdom of God moving toward sinners with an unconditional amnesty. He himself joined that movement from heaven to men, from the future into the present; in fact, he became the beachhead of this invasion by being guest of the most despised.

This very fellowship became the occasion for boisterous gaiety. Where John had acted like a boy inviting his playmates to stage a funeral, Jesus had acted like a boy calling them to join him in a wedding dance. The dancing took place with "tax collectors and sinners"; thus their eating and drinking seemed to outsiders like gluttony and drunkenness (7:31–34). *Until John, sorrow; since John, dancing.* And Luke considered all this a demonstration of a specific prophetic assignment from God.

Thus a conflict inevitably arose with the defenders of the law. *Until John, the Law and the Prophets; since John, the kingdom of God is preached* (16:16). The interpretation of this saying is extremely difficult, and no exegete can speak with total confidence about it. However, at the very least it reflects a view on the part of Luke as to how the prophetic activity of Jesus had changed the way in which forgiven sinners could and should deal with the Law and the Prophets, that is, with the revealed Scriptures. Jesus treated the Scripture in such a way as to arouse to murderous fury those whose task it was to defend it from travesty (6:11). He broke the Law by healing on the Sabbath and subsequently defended his action as lawful. He and his disciples broke the Law by harvesting grain on the Sabbath, and then appealed to the Law's account of David as precedent (6:1–10). In fact, he asserted that he had received authority to reinterpret the Law as he wished. His interpretation involved a radical paradox: the dawning of the kingdom produced a drastic change in the authority of Scripture, yet that change was in full accord with the promises of Scripture (a possible explanation of 16:17). Moses and all the prophets had anticipated the sending of a prophet who would announce the good news of the kingdom, and this would free men from such laws as that by which acts of mercy were forbidden on the Sabbath. Although any verbal definition of Luke's attitude here is precarious, we may say with some confidence: *until John, the Law and the Prophets; since John, a radical reinterpretation of the Scriptures.*

Something decisive had happened when Jesus, like Moses, had ascended the mountain for communion with God, and also when he, again like Moses, had descended from the mountain to disclose to the people the promises and the imperatives of the new dispensation (6:12–7:1). Whereas John appealed rather simply to the Scriptures in his call to repentance and warned of coming devastation on the proud, Jesus announced as already effective the very messianic blessedness and the penalties which John had anticipated (6:20–26). The actualities of such blessing and cursing were such as simultaneously to fulfill and to contradict Scripture, unless that Scripture were reinterpreted along the lines suggested by Jesus.

To return to the text which we have been using as a touchstone, let us quote the complete verse:

"The law and the prophets were until John; since then the good news of the kingdom of God is preached, and everyone enters it violently. But it is easier for heaven and earth to pass away than for one dot of the law to become void" (16:16–17).

For all its mysterious provocativeness, this text seems to justify three inferences.

1. The preaching of the good news marks the genuine termination of one epoch vis-à-vis the Scripture.
2. The violence of men in response to the good news is precipitated by this change in time zones.
3. In spite of appearances, this very preaching and violence celebrated an actual fulfillment of the Scripture.

The key questions are these: What is this violence? Who are the violent ones? How do they seek to enter the kingdom? How is the Law fulfilled in its apparent abrogation by the good news? The context in Luke indicates that the immediate audience for this riddle was the Pharisees, who were violently opposed to both John and Jesus. Moreover, the story underscores their self-justification and self-exaltation, sins which were grounded in their self-image as defenders of the Law and the Prophets. As they understood the Scriptures, they were righteous and these two prophets were blasphemous enemies of the Law. But Jesus declared that, since John's preaching, the Scriptures, as the scribes understood them, had become obsolete. Scribes should no longer rely on the Scriptures to serve as the basis for judging some men to be holier than others. In reaction, the Pharisees violently attacked the two prophets who had brought such "good news," (7:30; 19:47; 20:7, 14), believing that such violence was required by loyalty to the Law. Even so, the Gospel, as Jesus proclaimed it, would actually fulfill the Law, not destroy it. Both John and Jesus were charged with disclosing this fulfillment, and towards both, therefore, was the hostility of the Pharisees directed. If there was a distinction between the two, it was the work of Jesus which appeared to have attracted the greater violence because of his unrestrained exuberance in defying the Law. Luke thus became a witness to this hyperbolic paradox. In being superseded the Law was in fact fulfilled; by their violence the Pharisees had vindicated both the good news of the kingdom and the validity of the Law; likewise these two prophets had by their suffering testified to the power of the Gospel both to free men from the Law and to fulfill the Law. To the degree that Jesus was empowered to mediate the gifts of the new age (forgiveness, healing, liberation from demons, freedom from the Law, victory over death), to that degree the violence of his enemies would become the greater, but this, in turn would make the benefits of his passion the more redemptive.

In Luke's view it was not John but Jesus who had come as a prophet like Moses. It was Jesus' rejection and death which had fulfilled all the prophets and had marked the inception of God's kingdom. Thus interpreted, the violence mentioned in Luke 16:16 is comparable to the response given to Stephen's preaching (Acts 7:51–53) and to Jesus' parable of the tenants of the vineyard (Lk. 20:9–18).

All this may become clearer when we look at what is perhaps the most baffling enigma of all: Jesus' verdict on John, "Among those born of women none is greater than John; yet he who is least in the kingdom of God is greater than he" (Lk. 7:28). What are we to make of such a judgment? How interpret it? What clues do we have to Luke's understanding of it? The reader would be quite wrong to take the second half of the verse as motivated by the desire to diminish John's stature. Rather, the motivation of this whole passage is to oppose any inclination among Jesus' followers to downgrade this "messenger." Jesus does not hesitate to declare that John is a prophet and much more than a prophet. "None greater." Only when that epithet is fully accepted does the rest of the verse retain its hyperbolic force. Only in contrast to the greatest does the accent on the least make sense.

It would seem, however, that the central intent is not so much to compare two men, let us say John and Stephen, with greater honor being accorded to Stephen. Rather, there is an implicit contrast between all those "born of women," represented by the greatest, and all those born of the Spirit, represented by the least. This contrast coincides with the distinction before and after the coming of the kingdom, or before and after entrance into that new realm. The saying compares the greatest in one age to the least in another age, in such a way as to give a maximum tribute to the former and to underscore the vast reversal of standards which has been accomplished in the latter. Among those who prepared the way for the kingdom, none could be greater than John. But in fulfillment of his prophecy, the kingdom of God has dawned and Satan has been beaten. The emancipation declaration has been signed. "Greater than John" are the poor, the captives, the blind, the oppressed, the impotent who, baptized by the Spirit, have received forgiveness of sins, together with the other gifts of God in this new age. The paradoxical form of the saying may also indicate how the advent of the kingdom reversed all criteria of greatness. Not only does the new age give priority to the humblest, life within that age is organized around the law that the least become the greatest. Interpreted in this fashion, this verse in its context can stand as a summary of the ways in which the assignments given to these two prophets were similar, complementary, and yet distinctive.

This conception of Luke's attitude is, I think, in full harmony with the birth narratives. We find in them every indication of the greatness of John's commission as a prophet (1:76). His birth was ample evidence that "with God nothing is impossible" (1:37). Without any qualification, he is called "great before the Lord", fulfilling his vocation "in the spirit and power of Elijah" (1:14–17). In the literal sense, his work would mark the turning between two epochs. Mary's trip to Elizabeth before John's birth became both an effective testimony to John's destiny (similar to Jesus' judgment of him in 7:28) and a sign corroborating the angel's message to Mary in 1:36. Thus each prophet pointed to the other as divinely appointed and empowered. At the same time, without any invidious intent, the earliest predictions regarding the two prophets distinguished the two epochs, John's work being preparatory (1:17), giving anticipatory knowledge of the forgiveness that would come with the dawning of the day from on high (1:76—79), thus turning "many of the sons of Israel to the Lord their God" (1:16). Yet the same infancy narrative identifies the dawning of the new day with the reign of Jesus over the house of Jacob, a kingdom without end (1:33), a salvation for all generations, when the fulfillment of the covenant to Abraham would be accomplished, the hungry would be fed, the humble exalted, sinners forgiven, and the oppressed delivered from their enemies (1:48—55, 68—79). These are alternate ways of saying that the least in the kingdom of God are greater than John.[11]

The contrasts between these two prophets, John and Jesus, reenforce our earlier observations concerning Luke's portrait of Jesus as a prophet *like* Moses. Like Moses, Jesus had established a new covenantal basis for God's people and inaugurated a new epoch. In both, God had heard the cries of his people for deliverance and had redeemed them from captivity. Jesus had detected the signs of that liberation when he saw Satan fallen like lightning from heaven. From the dawning kingdom beyond judgment, beyond the Law and the Prophets, God had extended the miraculous gifts of the Spirit: joy, peace, forgiveness, fellowship, healing, courage, and hope. Peter's sermon in Acts 3 illustrated both the tranformations which God had wrought in raising up the prophet like Moses, and the rejection and violence with which the rulers of God's people had responded to the new deliverer.

Finally, let me compare Luke's portrait of Jesus with that of many contemporary scholars. The scholarly portraits are usually deficient in two ways. They make intelligible neither the volcanic explosion of popular excitement nor the geyser-like eruption of venom and hostility which greeted Jesus' ministry. They leave unexplained both the powerful lash and the equally powerful backlash. And what is true of scholarly portraits is even more true of the images of Jesus conveyed in contemporary preaching: bland, innocuous, noncontroversial. But this is not true of Luke's portrait of Jesus as a prophet like John and like Moses. Why are our pictures so anemic and so pale by contrast? Why has the sword of the Messiah become so dull? Let me mention three reasons, among many.

1. We lack effective analogies to use in the case of Jesus, prototypes like Moses and Abraham. Our community seems not to have a collective memory from which a stock of such analogies could be drawn. No longer is the Old Testament *our own* story, furnishing the basic language of our community. In this regard we do not even belong to the house of Israel in the period *before* John came preaching.

2. We have not experienced so deeply as did Luke either the longing for a new age or the gifts from such an age. Not having experienced anything worthy of the name repentance or forgiveness, it is nonsense to refer to the advent of the kingdom, as marking the most decisive change in the human situation. In this respect we are not prepared even to hear the prophetic call of John, to say nothing of Peter's announcement of a prophet like Moses.

3. If Luke is right in identifying the fulfillment of all prophecy in the sufferings of the Messiah; if he is right in viewing suffering as the experience common to the prophetic succession from Abel to Zechariah; if he is right in requiring all disciples of Jesus to share his passion, then it is surely true that, to understand such a vocation, modern disciples need the kind of training in suffering which Jesus provided for his followers. According to Luke, it was by way of sharing in the messianic sufferings that followers would apprehend the powerful presence of the new age in the redemptive activity of Jesus, raised up like Moses. In the next chapter we will examine this feature in the training of apostles toward becoming prophets like Jesus.

6

Every Christian who has received the Holy Spirit is now a prophet of the Return of Christ and by this very fact he has a revolutionary mission in politics: for the prophet is not one who confines himself to foretelling with more or less precision an event more or less distant; he is one who already "lives" it and already makes it actual and present in his own environment. [1]

THE APOSTLES AS PROPHETS LIKE JESUS

JESUS' VOCATION, as we have seen, connected his work to that of all the earlier prophets, but among them especially to Moses and to John the Baptist. That same vocation connected his work directly to the series of later prophets whom he would himself train and send out as his own apostles. In his first volume Luke describes their training and in the second their work. In both volumes their vocation was described as a continuation of Jesus' own baptism with the Spirit and fire.

PROPHECY AND APOSTLESHIP

First of all we should establish the fact that Luke thought of the Twelve as prophets, in the Gospel as apprentices and in Acts as fully authorized. Looking first at Acts, we may observe the thrust of the account of Pentecost. When we ask what it was that happened that seemed most significant to Luke, the answer must include, in one way or another, the baptism by fire and the Spirit of the 120 disciples of Jesus who had come up from Galilee with him. This baptism marked the gift of the Spirit from heaven. The act of prophesying was the strategic sign of that gift. Although the entire company received the gift, it was only Peter and the Twelve who were given the power to interpret what was happening. Such endowment with the prophetic gift was interpreted as the fulfillment of God's promise to Joel, as well as the prophecies of both John and Jesus. Nor should we neglect other prototypes and analogies. This story in Acts 2 suggests parallels between the initiation of the apostolic preaching and the sermon of Jesus in the Nazareth synagogue in fulfillment of Isaiah's prophecy. There are still other similarities between the work of the Spirit in Jerusalem and its activity in the infancy narratives. Still other nuances emerge when we recall the traditional Jewish views of Pentecost as the celebration of the giving of the Law to Moses on Sinai, that is, his commission as a revealer-prophet to Israel. Luke associated the anticipated redemption of Israel with the formation of a charismatic community created by the Spirit in solidarity with the people of God from the time of the covenant which God had sealed with Moses.

The Pentecost account suggests that, although not all Christian prophets were considered apostles, all apostles had received this baptism as prophets. E. Earle Ellis has shown that "every activity of the prophet . . . can also be ascribed by Luke to the apostle."[2] There were, of course, distinctions between the smaller and the larger groups of prophets, including this: "An apostle is simply a prophet who is sent as a missionary."[3] But in making this distinction we should not import into the idea of a missionary the modern notion of crossing geographical boundaries. The primary mission of the Twelve in Luke's view was to cross the frontier between heaven and earth, with a message from the Risen Lord to Israel. Of this Israel Jerusalem was the symbolic center. Any shift in assignment, as was the case with Peter and then Paul, required new guidance from heaven by way of a new vision and voice. All apostles were first prophets who remained dependent upon guidance from heaven through the Spirit as the mark of their vocation.

That Jesus closely associated the apostles with the prophets is made certain, at least in Luke's view, by the explicit decision in Luke 11:49–51: "I will send prophets and apostles to them." Although that assurance seems to visualize two separate groups, the rest of the saying reduces the two to one group, destined to become a single target of persecution: "some of whom they will kill and persecute, that the blood of all the prophets . . . may be required of this generation." Their blood would represent the blood of all prophets since Abel.[4] Again, in the Lucan debate with the persecutors of the church, the Christian prophets are visualized as eating with the fathers of Israel (all twelve tribes) in the kingdom of God (13:28–30), and Jerusalem is described as a city which continues to kill the prophets and to stone the messengers (apostles) sent to it (13:34). Here again, although there may be two distinct groups of charismatics, in Luke's mind they become one. Luke, following Q, clearly assumes the continuity between the persecutions of earlier prophets and the popular hatreds which would greet Jesus' own disciples. "So their fathers did to the prophets" (6:23). The absence of such hostility would indicate that they had become false prophets. "So their fathers did to the false prophets" (6:26). Again, in his conversation with his seventy-two messengers Jesus speaks of their visions and auditions as having been denied earlier to "prophets and kings" (10:24). Here we detect the tendency to treat the three images of apostles, prophets, and kings as virtually interchangeable (cf. 22:28–30). We do not contend that Luke was especially obsessed with prophetic terminology, but we do contend that of the three images, prophecy was the most basic and inclusive. It was by way of prophetic visions that the Twelve became authorized to represent Christ as his apostles. We will now trace in broad strokes the major steps taken by Jesus in training the Twelve as emissaries to Israel.

APPRENTICESHIP

The training began in earnest after Jesus had accepted the role announced by John and had made clear how John's call to repentance had opened the way for his own mission of forgiveness. Before this shift (8:1), the Twelve had remained in the background except at two points. The first of these incidents was the call of the four fishermen (5:1–11). The symbolic scenario for this episode accented Jesus' success in announcing the "word of God" to the prepared people. The eager response of this people to Jesus contrasted sharply with the futility of the night's fishing. When the fishermen obeyed his word, however, they were dumbfounded by the size of their catch, a forecast of later success. It is this promise of later success, so trustworthy that they left everything to follow him, which dominates the whole of the subsequent story in both of Luke's volumes.

The second episode was the selection of the Twelve (6:12–16). Here, too, the scenario is symbolic. As with Moses on Sinai, a contrast is apparent between the ascent to the mountain where through prayer Jesus was in direct rapport with God, and the descent to the level place where the revealer confronted a large circle of disciples and a great crowd of people who were eager to hear and to be healed. The naming of the Twelve on the mountain appears to be a divinely authorized response to the needs of this people, to this growing circle of disciples, and to the fury of the opponents whose murderous intent had already become apparent (6:11). The identification of Judas as traitor at the very outset also keeps the inevitable passion within the orbit of concern; these omens of betrayal and hostility provide a fitting setting for the giving of "living oracles" in which this second Moses proclaimed beatitudes on his disciples, woes on his enemies, and commands on how best to respond to persecution in every generation.

Chapter 8 recounts the story of the first missionary journey of the Twelve in company with Jesus, a journey in which he brought the good news of the kingdom to city after city. Travels on land and sea took them through Galilee and Gerasa, including both urban and rural areas. The fledgling prophets had the opportunity to observe at first hand both Jesus' teaching and his healing. He communicated the secrets of the kingdom to them (8:10), and made clear that they would be obliged to make those secrets more widely known (8:17). The storm at sea disclosed their immediate lack of faith, their deafness to the parable, their failure to grasp those secrets.

Their ineptness becomes particularly evident in the sequence of episodes which accompanied the departure and return of the Twelve on their first solo flight (9:1–50). For the first time the prophet like Moses authorized his twelve apprentices to announce the advent of the kingdom, to heal, and to drive out demons. As they went through the villages, Jesus' authority brought them a measure of success (cf. 22:35), though Luke as editor placed the greater emphasis on their failures. Several are specified, and it is implicit in the telling that these failures stemmed from a single source. The disciples were unable to feed the multitude in the desert, in part because they assumed that their resources of five loaves and two fish were inadequate (9:12–17). They failed to have such faith as would enable them to drive out demons from a helpless epileptic boy (9:38–42). They failed to understand the law of greatness (9:46–48) and the obligation to welcome all who exercised authority in their Master's name (9:49–50). In various ways these failures stemmed from their inability to understand the necessity of suffering on the part of both the Son of man (9:22, 44) and all who wanted to save their lives (9:23–26).

To Luke and his readers, these failures made all the more dramatic the successes of the Son of man. Luke understood the necessity of a victory over Satan such as had been won in the wilderness temptation, a victory whose key had been the acceptance of suffering, rejection, and death. It was this victory that enabled Jesus to feed the five thousand (the reference to the Twelve gathering the fragments in twelve baskets augured the gathering of Israel at his table after his death), and to heal the epileptic boy. But how could he communicate this lesson to the Twelve? This was the issue at the turning point in the drama. To communicate that lesson became a central objective of the prophet Jesus in everything that happened there-after. It required reiteration of the necessity that all prophets must perish. It required that Jesus set his face to go to Jerusalem, in company with these prophets-elect, so that progress toward that city might bring an advance in comprehension. In the end, however, the full induction of the Twelve into their prophetic role required a cycle of three visions of heavenly reality in which they would hear the word of God and be given power to obey it.

FIRST VISION: THE TRANSFIGURATION

The interdependence of three visions, as together constituting the ordination of the Twelve as prophets, has been hidden from us by the topical headings traditionally assigned to them: the transfiguration, the resurrection, Pentecost. As usually understood, the first two focus attention on what happened to Jesus, but Luke was more interested in what happened to the internes. I believe that we should read the transfiguration (9:28–36) as the first of those visions by which God established the vocation of the Twelve. Although this episode had an obvious significance for Jesus, giving a confirmation to his previous understanding of the exodus which he would accomplish at Jerusalem, Luke was far more concerned with the three men who were present as representatives of the Twelve. It is they whom Jesus had taken to the mountain for this rendezvous with God in prayer, they who had seen his heavenly glory and recognized his heavenly visitors, they who were caught up in fear "as they entered the cloud." Thereafter they could have no doubt that Jesus had received a divine mission designed to fulfill the promise to Moses of a prophet like Moses, coming like Elijah as prophet of the end-time.[5] The story reaches its climax in the failure of Peter to comprehend and in the voice that speaks out of the cloud. Peter's offer to build three booths (like the perversities described in vv. 41, 45, 46, and 49) reflects the desire "once more to bypass this indispensable factor, the cross."[6] God's voice identifies Jesus as "my Son, my Chosen" (i.e., the king-elect and redeemer of Israel); but, more decisively, God commands the three trainees to listen to him (cf. Dt. 18:15). The thrust of the vision is to assert as God's will the words of Jesus concerning the cross as the way of salvation for every prophet of the end-time (cf. 9:22–27, 44). How significant it is that only now *could* the journey to Jerusalem begin; also significant that it *must* begin now. Only with the second vision, after that journey has been completed, will these prophets fully and finally grasp the necessity of prophetic suffering and hence the inescapability of this command (24:25; against the background of 6:23; 11:47–51; 13:33–35; 22:14–22). The vision and the voice are focused on this staccato command to this specific audience in such a way as to underscore their subsequent silence, incomprehension, and perversity.

Much has been written about Luke's travel document and its organization (9:51–18:34). Although intermittent references to Jerusalem appear, the itinerary is by no means consistent as a step-by-step progression. I do not wish to contend that there is an orderly progression in terms of stages in the vocational training of the Twelve. What we find is an unorganized series of teachings and episodes which embody a fluctuating recurrence of attitudes in which the following convictions appear most frequently:

The Son of man must suffer (12:50; 13:33–34; 17:25; 18:31).

All who follow Jesus must accept the path of total self-denial (9:57–62; 12:4–12; 13:24; 14:25–33).

Although his emissaries are authorized to preach and to heal, they do not yet recognize the necessity of suffering (10:1–9).

Promises are issued to them which anticipate the time when that knowledge will become theirs (17:5; 18:29–30; 21:10–19).

Opponents who reject the Son of man and his representatives are assured of condemnation (10:10–16; 11:29–32, 39–46; 13:35; 17:26–30; 19:27, 41–44; 20:16; 21:20–24).

There is nothing distinctively Lucan in those attitudes, though Luke does take care to accent the fact that they are typical of the work of prophets. The Son of man recognized that his mission was controlled by the truth that a prophet cannot perish away from Jerusalem; it was this truth which defined the fire and baptism which he had been sent to earth to accomplish (12:49; 13:33). His envoys were described as men who have been enabled to see and to hear what prophets and kings have long hoped to see and to hear (10:23–24). Those who reject them will undergo as retribution "the blood of all the prophets, shed from the foundation of the world" (11:50). The desolation of a Jerusalem which kills Jesus is precisely the same as the final judgment on those who kill the prophets whom Jesus will later send to them (13:35; 11:49). All who choose to follow Jesus and his emissaries must bear their own crosses daily; it is this that entitles them to share the table in the kingdom of God with Abraham, Isaac, Jacob, and all the prophets (13:28–30). Rejection by God's people is thus shown to be the inescapable cost of fellowship with God's ambassadors. Yet Luke makes it clear that until the encounter with the Risen Lord, "they understood none of these things" (18:34).

This failure provided a major motif in the account of the Last Supper, where Jesus took the opportunity of the Passover seder to instruct the Twelve.[7] It is not impossible that Luke's arrangement of the extensive table talk in the Upper Room was influenced by his idea of Jesus as a second Moses engaged in the deliverance of Israel from bondage. It was with these prophets especially that Jesus had desired to eat this meal "before I suffer." Familiarity with the narrative may easily obscure for us the aspect of prophetic disclosure. What happens now happens in fulfillment of the predictions of scripture (22:22, 37) and also of Jesus' own predictions (e.g., 18:31–33). In the context of that double fulfillment, Jesus' selection of the host and of the guest room illustrates a kind of second sight. More significant still are his promises to eat again with the Twelve in the kingdom, his warnings regarding their betrayals, and his pledge of thrones judging the tribes of Israel.

Prophetic words are mirrored in prophetic deeds, in the signs that declared the significance of the event: the preparation of the Passover by the Twelve, the blessing and drinking of the cup, the breaking and eating of the bread, the waking and sleeping in Gethsemane. The whole past and the whole future were here telescoped into symbolic actions by which the covenant was sealed and the power of the kingdom assigned. Jesus' enemies were successful in arresting him, though not without betraying their fear of the people (22:2), their reliance on swordplay at night (vv. 49–51), and their craven use of money and subterfuge (v. 5). The moment of arrest demonstrated the truth of Jesus' declaration: "This is your hour and the power of darkness" (v. 53).

The continued transgressions of the disciples are also stressed as the fulfillment of prophecies (v. 37). The men continued, even at table, to mouth treasonable ideas of status and to betray equally traitorous ambitions (v. 24). In cowardice and fear they had bought two swords, thereby forfeiting their earlier independence and security (vv. 35–38).[8] All these sins were symbolized in their sleepiness during Jesus' greatest trial (v. 45). The reason for their betrayals continued to focus on failure to comprehend or to accept the necessity of suffering—his and theirs. For a moment Peter seems to have understood and accepted it, because he blurted out, "I am ready to go with you to prison and to death" (v. 33), but before dawn he too had swallowed the devil's lure.

Luke's account of Passover and the night following vindicated the predictions of prophet Jesus: his promise of betrayal and death in fulfillment of all the prophets; the disclosure of the "power of darkness" that had enslaved the rulers of the people; the stupidity of the Twelve in their refusal to comprehend the power of his weakness; the sealing of a covenant with them which named them as future judges and kings of Israel. Here Luke describes both the failure of his earlier pedagogical efforts to train them as prophets to continue his vocation and the renewed promise of success still to come. The emergence of that success is the chief thrust of Luke's account of the next encounter between Jesus and the Twelve, the story usually labeled "the resurrection of Jesus."

SECOND VISION: THE RESURRECTION

There is much to be learned by reading this story as the second of three visions required for the commissioning of the Twelve as prophets. Luke's own way of viewing this event is suggested by Peter's sermon in Acts 10, in which a number of typical Lucan accents lie near the surface of the text.

> "They put him to death by hanging him on a tree; but God raised him on the third day and made him manifest, not to all the people but to us who were chosen by God as witnesses, who ate and drank with him after he rose from the dead. And he commanded us to preach to the people" (vv. 39–42).

The last chapter in Luke's Gospel could well be labeled "the creation of witnesses," for here the accent falls upon the manifestation of the risen Lord to God's chosen ambassadors—"not to all but to us." The story fuses together that vision, audition, command, and sign which enabled them to become witnesses (a term which in Acts connotes prophets). God's action is seen as overcoming Jesus' rejection by Israel in such a way as to send witnesses back to that very nation, the people to whom Jesus had been sent. This same action is comprehended as a fulfillment of all the earlier prophets and as an offer of a new promise, the forgiveness of sins through the name of this risen King. The meal which he celebrated anew with the apostles (24:42–43) both fulfilled his earlier promises to them (22:14–16) and assured for them his continuing though invisible presence. Peter's sermon in Acts 10 thus epitomized the Lucan understanding of the role of the risen Lord in the making of witnesses. The fulfillment of his own vocation reached its dramatic climax in the inception of theirs.

When we examine Luke 24 from this standpoint, two strategic questions emerge: What deficiency in their previous training does this chapter underscore? How do the events remove that deficiency? To answer both questions we must observe those themes which recur in all three encounters of the risen Jesus: with the women, the Emmaus couple, and the larger company. In each case there is an explicit rebuke of their earlier mistake. The rebuke of the women:

> "Why do you seek the living among the dead? Remember how he told you, while he was still in Galilee, that the Son of man must be delivered into the hands of sinful men, and be crucified, and on the third day rise" (vv. 6–7).

The rebuke of the Emmaus couple:

> "O foolish men, and slow of heart to believe all that the prophets have spoken! Was it not necessary that the Christ should suffer these things and enter into his glory?" (vv. 25–26)

The rebuke of the entire company:

> "These are my words which I spoke to you, while I was still with you, that everything written about me in the law of Moses and the prophets and the psalms must be fulfilled. . . . that the Christ should suffer and on the third day rise from the dead" (vv. 44–46).

The repetition makes the point entirely clear. Without this final lesson in the necessity of suffering, the training of these witnesses would have been wholly inadequate. Until the death and the appearances of the Risen Lord, it had proved impossible for them to learn this lesson, with all its implications. But their encounter with him conveyed such a vision and audition of God's will as to clinch simultaneously both his earlier prophecies and their commission as witnesses. The evangelist was more concerned to clarify their future vocation than to speculate concerning changes in the Lord's body.

This is made entirely clear in the remaining promise of Jesus:

> "You are witnesses of these things. And behold, I send the promise of my Father upon you; but stay in the city until you are clothed with power from on high" (vv. 48–49).

The fulfillment of one promise here leads to the issuing of another, while all the promises are subordinated to a single goal, "that repentance and forgiveness of sins should be preached in his name to all nations" (v. 47). Whose name? The name of "the prophet mighty in deed and word," anointed to redeem Israel, "the prophet like Moses." His separation from them and his ascension appear to have been linked to his immediate blessing and to the subsequent fulfillment of his promise. From heaven he would be in a position to send his promised power and to dispense forgiveness of sins whenever they preached in his name. For them as prophets, christophanies would tend to replace the theophanies of the earlier prophets. Jesus' vocation would continue in theirs whenever they appealed to the power of his name.

I do not, of course, wish to reduce the significance of the stories of their encounters with the risen Lord to this single function, but I do contend that in Luke's intention the basic function lay in this area of the training of prophetic spokesmen. This series of visions, auditions, covenantal promises and demands, by fulfilling earlier predictions and by issuing new assurances, served as a decisive reinterpretation of Scripture; it conveyed new understandings of Jesus' earlier work and a definitive assignment for their own future work, including a definition of tenure and audience. Hereafter they would know with confidence not only that he was "a prophet mighty in deed and word" but also that he was "the one to redeem Israel" not in spite of his rejection and death but because of it (24:21, 25–27).[9]

THIRD VISION: PENTECOST

The stories of the risen Lord constitute an introduction to Luke's second volume as well as a conclusion to his first. There are subtle shifts in perspective, and the intended force of these shifts emerges as soon as we focus attention on the apostolic witnesses (Acts 1). Hereafter the understanding of his passion is no longer argued but assumed; in fact it now becomes an essential part of their own message to Israel. Reiterating his promise of the Spirit-baptism, Jesus now gave them instructions for the remaining period until that promise should be fulfilled. Having convinced them of his identity as Israel's redeemer, he now replied to their bewilderment as to times and seasons by making their own mission to the end of the earth an essential step toward Israel's redemption. Now, the reference to his ascension into heaven has a new function; whereas in the Gospel it had emphasized the heavenly source of his blessing and power, it now provided the future horizon for their mission. Beyond the promise of the descent of the Spirit which would initiate their mission they now receive from heaven the promise of the return of their commander-in-chief from heaven. As soon as their work should be empowered by the Spirit, this promise of his return would define the tenure and goal of their stewardship.

The only other matter which Luke viewed as unfinished business which had to be handled before Pentecost was the choice of a new twelfth prophet, to accord with the number of the brethren (the 120 of Acts 1:15) and with the number of the tribes of Israel. Not all the prophets became apostles to Israel, but all twelve apostles must be anointed as prophets, selected by the Lord, and empowered by the Spirit to serve as prophets and kings (Lk. 10:22; 22:28). The selection of Matthias as an "eyewitness" to join the other eleven "ministers of the word" is strategically located by Luke as the only event intervening between the ascension and Pentecost. Luke was keenly aware of the symbolic weight of this event. It reinforced the strategic importance of the selection and training of the Twelve as narrated in the Gospel (6:13). It completed the number of rulers of Israel promised at the Supper (22:30). It opened the way for a Pentecostal ultimatum to Israel by those twelve "prophets and kings".

Biblical interpreters have long recognized the symbolism of the number twelve as referring to the twelve sons of Jacob-Israel, the twelve patriarchs and archetypes of the tribes which constituted the whole of the covenant people. The established view, as Jeremias has reconstructed it, held that only two and a half tribes had survived the fall of the Northern kingdom in 722 B.C.[10] Faithful Jews anticipated the restoration and gathering of all twelve tribes as a sign of the end-time and as a work of the prophet like Moses. So the same

Jesus who had called the Twelve must now select a replacement for Judas before these prophets would be in a position to announce "the last days" to Israel. M.D. Goulder adds a further motif to this symbolism. Because ten men could form a synagogue, the group of 120 indicated the presence in the church of a synagogue from each of the twelve tribes.[11] The story is thus an excellent illustration of the principle of *pars pro toto* which, as E. Cassirer has demonstrated, governs all mythic thinking. "The part does not merely represent the whole, or the specimen its class; they are identical with the totality to which they belong, not merely as mediating aids to reflective thought, but as genuine presences which actually contain the power, significance and efficacy of the whole."[12]

The choice of Matthias also accords with Luke's understanding of the calling of prophets. Their calling represents not only their own volition but the will of God. Accordingly, the story leaves the ultimate decision as to Judas' replacement to the heavenly Jesus, to whom the Eleven continued to have access by prayer. Jesus' original intention thus triumphed over human defection: the Twelve will do his work under his authority and according to his purpose. This purpose is not so much to provide rulers for the congregations as to furnish witnesses to testify to what has happened on earth and in heaven between the baptism of John and the ascension of Jesus.[13] Matthias had already received the requisite visions and auditions; he must now receive that specific assignment to four tasks which comprised the unique prophetic work of the Twelve vis-à-vis Israel: apostleship, governance, service, and witness (Acts 1:20, 22, 25). The crucifixion had not cancelled Jesus' mission to Israel. Through God's governance it had made possible the restoring of the kingdom to Israel, a quite unexpected answer to the disciples' question in Acts 1:6. The twelve could now testify on the basis of their own experience that the death of Jesus had been no "messianic catastrophe" but "a decisive condition for the completion of God's design for mankind."[14] So construed, the selection of Matthias is in direct line with the vocation of Jesus in volume one, and a necessary preparation for the mission of the Twelve to Israel in volume two.

To understand Luke's account of Pentecost we should avoid the misconceptions involved in the notion of this event as "the birthday of the church" and should focus attention on two elements: the completion of the preparation of these Twelve to serve as missionary-prophets, and the beginning of the work by which the risen Lord restored the kingdom to Israel. In this event, the prophecies of Moses, Isaiah, Joel, John the Baptist, and Jesus were fulfilled when the whole company of disciples was baptized by the Spirit. They were granted a vision of the descent from heaven of the Spirit and fire, a third vision which completed the divine calling which had been initiated at the transfiguration and continued at the resurrection. Having been called by Jesus (Lk. 6:12 ff.), having been inducted into heavenly secrets (9:28–36), having been granted authority to proclaim the kingdom (10:21 ff.), having become recipients of the covenant (22:29 f.), having been at last convinced of the necessity of the passion (24:46), they were now empowered by the Spirit's fire to promise the gift of the Spirit to all who repented. Made prophets by this gift, they were enabled to reinterpret Scripture in the light of this specific "sign" of messianic fulfillment and to proclaim with authority: "Let all the house of Israel know . . ." (Acts 2:36). Their work produced "fear" in every soul, and through them many wonders and signs were done. The resurrection encounter had eliminated their chief disqualification (their blindness to the necessity of suffering); the descent of the Spirit now provided them with the last essential qualification: power to witness, the courage to call Israel to repentance for crucifying their Messiah and to promise to the same Israel forgiveness of sins and the gift of the Spirit. In this way the account of Pentecost provided a striking parallel to the baptism of Jesus; *here* the Twelve received their share in the vocation which he had received *there*. They now fully entered the goodly fellowship of the prophets, from Abel to Moses to John to Jesus to Peter. As Luke told the story of Pentecost, he saw embodied in it the fulfillment of many earlier prophecies, and none was more decisive than God's promise to Moses, since Israel had for generations celebrated at Pentecost the giving of the Law to Moses. In fulfilling that promise (Acts 3:22), God had fulfilled the promises Jesus had given to the Twelve and had enabled the Twelve to announce to Israel the inception of the "last days." Only after Pentecost could Peter truly announce the redemption promised to Moses in Deuteronomy 18:15.

This gives special importance to the Israel which Luke pictures as the audience present at this Pentecost.[15] They were Jews who had come "from every nation under heaven." In describing this audience Luke used the term "the multitude" (*plēthos*) without further qualification (2:6). By this he signified the full assembly or gathering of Israel in the last days, a usage found also among the Essenes of Qumran.[16] Moreover, by the symbol of tongues-speaking Luke was able to assert that the whole of Israel, though scattered abroad in every nation, was able to hear this new witness to the mighty works of God, each in his own tongue. Therefore "the whole house of Israel" (2:36) was for the first time able to see and to hear the promised salvation, these earthly signs of heavenly redemption. Here was fulfillment of God's promise to Moses. Those who repented and were baptized did in fact now receive the Holy Spirit as gift (the 3,000 of Acts 2:41) and became the restored Israel, a fulfillment of the promise that all God's people would become prophets. Those who refused to listen were "destroyed from the people" (3:23). It was Israel and not the church which served as the audience of the Pentecost prophecy. In one sense all the followers of Jesus (the 120 persons of 1:15) became on this occasion the recipients of the Spirit and fire and therefore God's witnesses to Israel. In another sense, the function of the Twelve, with Peter as spokesman, became all the more decisive. As divinely authorized interpreters of Scripture and of these signs, they could, with power derived from the Risen Lord, issue ultimate demands and promises, and provide that "teaching and fellowship" (2:42) which established continuity between this Israel and the Israel which had repented at the preaching of John. All this is to say that there are significant links between the Pentecost story and virtually every episode in Luke's Gospel, beginning with the angel's visit to Zechariah. Moreover in Luke's view the vocation of Jesus was continued and fulfilled in the vocation of every one who would later be baptized in his name (2:38). The two stories as told in the two volumes are really a single story. "The break between them is not of such decisive importance as that between the period of the Law and the Prophets and the period in which the gospel is preached."[17]

We may now sum up the major changes accomplished in the twin events of resurrection and Pentecost by utilizing the same formula as before: "until . . . since then."

UNTIL the resurrection the disciples had been unable to understand or to accept the scriptural provisions concerning the messiah's suffering;

SINCE then they were able to understand, and after Pentecost to expound, those provisions.

UNTIL the resurrection they had been unable to accept suffering and death as their own earthly destiny;

SINCE then they were given the ability and were enabled to announce that destiny as requisite for all believers.[18]

UNTIL Pentecost they had not received the baptism of the Spirit;

SINCE then they were so baptized and were enabled to offer that baptism to others.

UNTIL Pentecost their power as prophets had been limited;

SINCE then they were enabled both to perform and to interpret many signs and wonders.

UNTIL Pentecost they had not been fully authorized to announce the forgiveness of sins in Jesus' name;

SINCE then that authorization came into force.

UNTIL Pentecost Gethsemane had served as sign of their cowardice, impatience, drowsiness;

SINCE then they became models of courage, endurance, wakefulness.

UNTIL Pentecost Jesus' predictions of betrayal had been fully in force;

SINCE then his promise of thrones came into operation.

UNTIL Pentecost, they had received instruction in the secrets of the kingdom of God;
SINCE then they became qualified revealers of those secrets ("There is no secret that shall not be made known" [Lk. 8:17, 10]).

UNTIL Pentecost they had been primarily hearers of God's word;
SINCE then the test for them became the doing of that word.

UNTIL Pentecost they had been subject to the commands of the Son of man on earth;
SINCE then they became subject to the commands of the risen and returning Lord.

UNTIL Pentecost their mission had been limited in space (Galilee, Samaria) and in time (his arrival in Jerusalem);
SINCE then it expanded in space (all nations, beginning in Jerusalem) and in time (until his return).

UNTIL Pentecost the future horizon for their discipleship had been the promised descent of the Spirit;
SINCE then that horizon shifted to their Master's promised return as Judge and Redeemer.

In the above summary we have focused attention on the revealer-prophets. Luke also displays a strong interest in the Spirit-guided vocation of the entire community. The account of the growth of "the word of God" reflects Luke's view that "a disciple who does not possess the Spirit is a contradiction in terms."[19] Each congregation was oriented to the production and reception of prophetic utterance, each believer becoming a witness to the advent of the times of refreshing. So we append another epitome: until Pentecost the community of the poor had been seen as recipients of the gospel; after Pentecost they became channels of the power of the Spirit.

So decisive and so comprehensive were the changes accomplished in these two events that Lucan readers may well ask what is the need for successors to the Twelve or for any extension of their mandate.

The need for such successors is one thing when we view the Twelve as apostles, with a commission primarily designed to provide governors for the church. It is quite different when we view them as prophets, continuing that succession in which it is an essential characteristic that each contemporary fulfillment becomes the occasion for a new promise. This aspect of Luke's perspective may be illustrated by four instances of prophetic visions subsequent to Pentecost.

PROPHETIC GUIDANCE OF THE MISSION

The first such instance developed in response to a changed audience and a new set of needs. In Acts 6 the audience shifted both in numbers and character: more numerous now, it was composed of both Hebrews and Hellenists. This inclusion of the first "minority" created difficulties in the daily distribution of food. The Twelve, who conceived of prophetic preaching as their primary assignment, were prompted to propose the appointment of seven deacons. These seven, however, on being ordained, immediately began to act like prophets. They became recipients of faith, grace, wisdom, power, and the Spirit—the recognized marks of the prophet. Moreover, the great signs and wonders which they performed provoked both the typical awe and the typical rejection. It was after Stephen had interpreted this rejection as a fulfillment of God's promise to Moses that they demonstrated the cogency of that very promise by stoning him. This, in turn, occasioned for him a typical prophetic vision of heaven, the glory of God, and the powerful Son of man; he uttered an authentic prayer for the forgiveness of his persecutors, a prayer whose power was verified in the later vision of Christ to one of those same persecutors. Luke discerned in this episode a genuine succession in the divine calling of prophets: the Son of man, the twelve apostles, Stephen, Paul.

Luke also traced another line of succession from the prophet Stephen to the prophet Philip. Ordained a deacon with Stephen, Philip disclosed all the marks of a prophet: the witness to the Risen

Christ, exorcisms, healings, an outburst of joy (8:6–8), remarkable instances of conversion and baptism (8:12–13), alertness to the leadings of an angel, ability to reinterpret Isaiah, identification of the "sheep led to the slaughter" with Jesus. The matter of special note to Luke was the fact that Philip was directed by the Spirit to carry the good news to two very different auditors, first to Simon the magician and then to the Ethiopian cabinet minister. In his work with them, Philip performed tasks identical with those assigned to the apostles, with the prophetic result: "the word of the Lord grew."

When Luke told of the persecution of the Jerusalem church following Stephen's martyrdom, he appended a comment which I believe is usually misconstrued by exegetes: "They were all scattered throughout the region of Judea and Samaria, except the apostles" (Acts 8:1). Why were the apostles excepted? Inasmuch as the text does not say, readers are bound to speculate. Were they exempt from the persecution? That is by no means certain. Did they limit their work to Jerusalem? If so, why should Luke immediately recount a journey by two of them to Samaria (8:14–25) including gospel preaching? Why did Luke exempt the apostles from the scattering? The usual answer is to say that they were too conservative, too cautious, too near in theological position to the Jerusalem authorities to attract their venom. That answer is possible, but it remains conjectural. Moreover, it is hardly consonant with Luke's editorial convictions. A conjecture more congenial to his stance would express almost the opposite conclusion. The Twelve remained in Jerusalem *in spite of* the persecution because of their obedience to Jesus' commission. They had been appointed to rule over the twelve tribes by carrying the gospel to them. The symbolic center of these tribes was Jerusalem. They had finally learned the difficult lesson of the passion that no prophet should perish outside of Jerusalem and that in that city the blood of all the prophets would be "required of this generation" (Lk. 11:45–51; 14:31–35). In his account of persecution in Jerusalem, therefore, Luke may have simply seen the fulfillment of their vocational covenant with their Master.

Still a third development which Luke describes at great length is the innovation of the mission to Gentiles by one of the Twelve who had initially been assigned to Israel. We should read the story of Peter and Cornelius (10:1–11:18; 15:6–11) as a clear instance of prophetic revelation. It is of course true that this episode tells of the conversion not of Cornelius but of Peter.[20] It is even nearer the mark to say that it really recounts not so much the conversion of Peter as a step in the *prophetic guidance* of the Judean churches by the Spirit acting through Peter. In telling the story, Luke omits virtually none of the marks of prophecy: prayer, fasting, hunger, a heavenly vision interpreted by a heavenly voice, a command for immediate action, the coincidence of heavenly command with human dilemma, the reinterpretation of Scripture, the specific instructions conveyed by the Holy Spirit, the perception by the prophet of the audience to whom he is commissioned, the proclamation of the Word, the call to faith, the promise of forgiveness, the gift of the Spirit, the speaking with tongues in praise and thanksgiving, the baptism of believers, the fulfillment of all the prophecies, opposition to the new precedents, their validation by the Spirit and its witnesses. This long narrative is nothing less than a full-scale portrait of a Christian prophet in action. In this case, the vision is the fifth in the series in which Peter shared. The five include his initial call at the lake (Lk. 5:1–11), the disclosure of the transfigured Jesus, the encounter with the risen Lord, the release of Pentecostal power, and now the extension of the gospel to Gentiles.

PAUL AS PROPHET

Before completing the roster of visions, we must include the calling of Paul as a prophet, concerning which Luke provides three accounts.[21] It is entirely misleading to call this event the conversion of Paul; rather it is his calling to be a witness to the risen Lord and to reveal to Gentiles the will of God and the name of Jesus. As evidence we merely list those features in the stories which characterize prophetic "ordinations": Luke thought of Paul as an instrument chosen by the risen Christ "to carry my name before the Gentiles and kings and the sons of Israel" (9:15). The three accounts agree in accenting as the immediate setting Paul's violent campaign against the Christains, motivated by his loyalty to Scripture. They tell of a vision of Christ, a light shining from heaven, and a voice identified as that of Jesus. This voice disclosed Jesus' solidarity with the targets of Paul's hatred. It corrected Paul's previous attitudes toward the death of Jesus and, in doing so, forced him to revise his understandings of Scripture. The voice issued commands which conveyed both immediate instructions and ultimate tasks in serving as Christ's spokesman before a specified audience for the rest of Paul's life—suffering for the name being specified as an essential feature of that task. The fullest account of this mandate appears in the third instance; here Paul tells how he had been appointed envoy to the Gentiles with instructions virtually the same as those which the Twelve had received for Israel (26:17 f.). The three accounts of his heavenly vision differ in certain aspects of the scenario: Paul's blindness and its cure, the prophetic role of Ananias, the observance of prayer and fasting, the mode of the Spirit's descent, the calling on the name, the significance of baptism and the laying on of hands. One can become engrossed in analyzing these variables, but it is far more important to recognize the constants. All the features in all three accounts conform to Luke's notions of how Christ called prophets to disclose the secrets of heaven.

It is necessary, of course, to recognize sharp contrasts between Luke's view of this event and Paul's own. Even though I am at the moment concerned only with Luke's outlook, I have no wish to minimize those contrasts. Yet it is unwise to deny several important coincidences between the two. In Galatians, for example, Paul himself stressed his own prior role as a persecutor. Incidentally this destroys the contention that appearances of the risen Christ were limited to believers and followers; rather it suggests that they were limited to those whom Jesus wished to send as prophets and apostles. According to both Galatians and Acts, Paul's commission came to him by way of the revelation of Jesus Christ (Gal. 1:12 ff.). That revelation impelled a radical reinterpretation of Scripture, focused now on the significance of Jesus' rejection and crucifixion. As an expression of God's grace and forgiveness, that revelation had transformed Paul's conception of himself: he had been set apart from his birth for a task which must now monopolize all his energies and must express itself in daily dying with Christ. The call opened the way to continuing guidance by revelation from the same source (Gal. 2; 2 Cor. 12) and released his power to work many signs and wonders. To Paul as to Luke the manifestation of the risen Lord was comparable (with certain qualifications) to earlier manifestations to his predecessors (I Cor. 15). Thereafter he felt constrained both to live and to walk by the Spirit (Gal. 5:25).

Our conviction that Luke included Paul within the succession of prophets does not depend on whether he also viewed Paul as an apostle, an issue that is vigorously debated. Probably a majority of scholars deny that Luke admitted Paul to that echelon, in spite of the explicit designation of Paul and Barnabas as apostles in two verses (Acts 14:4, 14). Here I vote with the minority who believe that in Luke's eyes Paul was an apostle. It may be true that Luke pictured "a closed college" of twelve "cardinals" sitting in Jerusalem as governors of the early church; but, if so, I think the stress upon the number twelve corresponds to the symbolic demands of a mission addressed *to Israel*. That did not mean that Luke denied Christ's power to appoint and to anoint other apostles who would be assigned *to Gentiles*. However, quite apart from that debatable point, I want here to stress my conviction that, while not all prophets were apostles, all apostles were prophets, and that, when we recapture Luke's understanding of the prophetic succession, this diminishes the dogmatic weight of any contrast between the Twelve and the other messengers whom the risen Christ sent to reveal his name and his power.[22]

In this respect it is significant that in Luke's account it was in connection with the mission to Gentiles that conflict developed between the other apostles and Paul. But it is even more significant that this conflict was resolved by reference not to apostolic prerogatives but to prophetic reliance by all the apostles and elders upon the guidance of the Holy Spirit. We have already mentioned the fourth vision of heaven vouchsafed to Peter as a missionary prophet in Acts 10, compelling him to baptize a Gentile centurion. It is a sign of Luke's editorial perspective that he located this episode almost immediately *after* Paul's commissioning as an apostle to the Gentiles (9:15) and immediately *before* the opening of the mission to the Gentiles in Antioch (11:20). Luke also takes care to show how the same prophets who responded to the presence of the Holy Spirit among the Gentiles also responded to the call by Agabus for help to the Judean brethren (11:20–30). At every step in Luke's story it had been the Holy Spirit's guidance of the prophets which had impelled the work among new audiences (e.g., Acts 13:1–3). So at the Jerusalem council it was an appeal to this guidance of missionary prophets which had resolved the conflict, so that "the apostles and the elders" were impelled to write "it has seemed good *to the Holy Spirit* and to us" (15:28) and to send their letter by the hand of two prophets (15:32). In short, if their work as apostles assigned by Christ to different audiences had produced conflicts, their subjection as prophets to guidance by the Holy Spirit resolved those conflicts and produced joy and peace (15:31–33). Luke may have minimized those conflicts, but if he did so, it was as a testimony to his conception of the power of prophecy, including Jesus' prophecies in the Gospel (5:10; 22:28–30; 24:44–49) and in Acts (1:8; 11:16). Even more it was an expression of his understanding of the vocation of Jesus as a prophet raised up like Moses to redeem God's people and to bless all the families of the earth (Acts 3:22–26).[23]

Just as it did not diminish reverence for Jesus to identify him as that prophet, so it did no damage to the authority of the apostles to describe their work in prophetic categories: "I will send them prophets and apostles some of whom they will kill and persecute" (Lk 11:49). Luke's organization of the traditions in both volumes is fully consistent with that prophecy. This may not seem to apply to the long circumstantial accounts of Paul's trip to Rome, although even the bizarre details of that trip verified, albeit in naive ways, Paul's gifts of charismatic discernment of hearts and his power to foretell the future (27:9, 22–26, 31, 34–36; 28:5, 8). However that may be, Paul's vocation as a prophet comes clearly to the fore in the closing paragraphs of the Acts. Here Paul disclosed how Christ had fulfilled the hope of Israel, and he supported this disclosure with a reinterpretation of Scripture that provoked a dissension with Jews, which he explained in terms of the Holy Spirit's voice in Isaiah (parallel to Jesus' sermon at Nazareth). It was against this background that Paul defended the Gentile mission and witnessed to the presence of the kingdom as "the salvation of God." Luke saw alike in Paul's chains, in the blindness of Israel, and in the response of the Gentiles a fulfillment of Jesus' prophecy, along with many other Christian prophecies.

Beginning with the prophecy of Zechariah, the father of John, each witness had announced the fulfillment of Scripture. After the word came to John, each spokesman had called men to repent and to produce deeds worthy of repentance. After the baptism of Jesus, the Holy Spirit had become active in many various ways, both hidden and revealed. From the time of his temptation, Jesus had recognized that in the struggle with the devil, only the acceptance of weakness, hunger, and humility could provide a channel for God's power. Beginning with the prophetic disclosures of Easter, the disciples knew "that the Christ must suffer and that, by being the first to rise from the dead, he would proclaim light" (Acts 26:23). From Pentecost on, the witnesses received power to baptize believers with the same Spirit. From the time of the visions of Paul and Peter and of the apostles and elders in Jerusalem, Christ's choice of the Gentiles had been authenticated. So Luke recognized every spokesman of the Most High, from Zechariah to Paul, as a prophet; in fact, the charismatic gifts had been so freely poured out at Pentecost on the whole people, that all had become prophets, telling each in his own tongue the story of what God had done.

The gift of the Spirit thus created an absolute solidarity in a single vocation, coextensive with the community of faith. The gift simultaneously enabled that community to discern the common tasks and to recognize the distinctive assignments given by the risen Lord to those who had accompanied him since the baptism of John, those to whom he had appeared during the forty days, and those whom he continued to call whether in Damascus or Antioch or Rome. Some members of that succession received quite unique gifts; others received the power to interpret those gifts. All stood under the Messiah's promise of judgment and salvation to come, when he would return to his estate and call all servants to an accounting (Acts 1:11). Until then each servant had his own task, though all were engaged in one way or another with the proclamation of forgiveness of sins to all nations (Lk. 24:47). Each prophet maintained solidarity with the community as a whole and yet each had a distinct assignment; the same solidarity bound the apostles to their Lord.

Their likeness to Jesus could be described in various terms: a vision of heaven that conveyed authority, baptism in the Spirit, the use of his power and name, the working of signs and wonders, the forgiveness of sins, the feeding of his sheep. If asked to single out the two most essential bonds, I would reply: first, a situation in which their witness plunged the speakers into hostility and persecution to such a degree that their passion story reflected his. Second, a readiness to apply to that situation an ethic "grounded on nothing but response to the unmediated reality of God."[24] Such is the heritage of the prophets to whom Luke traced the traditions which he incorporated in both volumes. Whether and how this succession of prophets continues into our own day will be the concern of our final chapter.

7

*[There is a] fundamental dialectic between the wit-
ness of Scripture and classical Christian tradition,
on the one side, and the fabric of our daily lives, on
the other. Rediscovering this dialectic lies . . . at
the center of what it means to be called to be a professor of theology. . . . The certainty of our hope lies
in the fact that this theological vocation depends ultimately not on our grasp of it, but rather on God's
faithfulness to his promise of life in Jesus Christ.
Therefore this vocation shall never fall to the
ground.* [1]

THE PROPHETIC VOCATION
TODAY

THE EARLIER CHAPTERS have surely pro-
voked many objections, or at least reservations, among the readers.
Some readers will no doubt question the accuracy of my readings of
the historical evidence. Did Luke portray Jesus' vocation as so fully
akin to that of John? Did Luke so consciously and carefully present
Jesus as a prophet like Moses? Are we justified in interpreting Luke's
two volumes as an account of the training of apprentice seers and
exorcists—calling, transfiguration, resurrection, Pentecost? These
questions are inescapable for all who take seriously the tasks of a historian. It may very well be that in concentrating upon the prophetic
language and vocation I have in fact misread Luke. I do not think so,
yet others must give their own verdict. I trust that such a verdict

will not fall into a semantic trap, a trap set by the term *prophet*. Luke did not frequently employ that term, and I do not wish to rest my entire case upon its use. Charismatic gifts and tasks are not easily reduced to verbal counters that carry fixed meanings. Luke was dealing with vocational actualities, which stemmed from specific calls and commissions, and which produced a distinctive consciousness and language. We have tried to comprehend that language as a whole, and if some other word than *prophet* seems more accurate, it should by all means be adopted. For example, the term *charismatic ministry* might be preferable were it not so distorted by recent journalism.

It is true that many features of Luke's perspective create uncertainties for his readers, and not least for expert historians. But the presence of several features can hardly be contested. We can be quite certain that he was writing primarily for readers in his own day and that he had multiple and various intentions in addressing them.[2] We can also be confident that in his mind there had been a succession of prophets from Abel to Paul, a succession linked together by divine purpose and human suffering. With perhaps less confidence we may suppose that Luke pictured that succession as continuing beyond the death of Paul into the churches of his own day. If he had supposed that guidance by the Spirit had terminated with Paul, the message of his two volumes would have been aborted and he would have had little to say to Theophilus. If we may assume that Luke believed in continuing charismatic guidance of his own churches, we can infer that this guidance would have entailed a double set of gifts: on the one hand, Spirit-filled seers, revealers, healers, interpreters, and on the other hand, Spirit-led watchers and listeners—men and women who, in seeing the signs, were led to faith and who, in hearing the word, were led to obedience. This is the very point of Luke's stress on the crowds who came out to hear the word and to see the signs, and who in response to the message became disciples of the prophet like Moses. The evangelist assumed that this double set of charismatic gifts was still active in the churches of his own day.[3]

Since this was true for Luke, his example impels us to pose such questions as the following: Are those gifts equally essential to twentieth-century churches? Does the same prophetic vocation continue among us? If so, does Luke help us to recognize the authentic signs, whether of charismatic speaking or of equally charismatic listening? These are genuine and not rhetorical questions in that negative as well as positive answers may be correct. The questions are also genuine in that the presence of such signs and gifts depends ultimately on a God who can hide as well as disclose his powerful presence. Moreover, it is obvious that there may well be multiple answers in view of the multiple needs of multiple audiences. Even so, Luke's example impels us to reflect on these questions. Are there in America today successors to the prophets, or, if we cannot and should not name names, is there a continuation of their distinctive vocation? If so, where may it be found? And where may we discern the twin gift of hearing-and-obeying what these prophets are saying?

We all recognize a parallel problem, that of locating the authentic successors of the *apostles*. The contorted dogmatic and denominational controversies over that subject have bestowed "a conflict of interest" on all exegetical judges. However, exegetes are relatively free from that conflict in dealing with the prophetic succession, since this matter, though no less important and no less complex, has not been complicated by the ecclesiastical institutionalization of the prophetic office.

It may, of course, be wrong to expect from Luke any substantial help in dealing with this succession today, since our modern technocratic society did not come within the horizons of his world. He had neither concern nor capacity for dealing with it, and we would be utterly wrong either to force modern readers to step into his world or to transport him into ours. On the other hand, it would be just as wrong to erect an impenetrable curtain between the two epochs, for this would mean that all people become helpless captives of the calendar. Without ignoring cultural and chronological distances, we may find more help from his thinking than is usually expected. At the very least we can let Luke remind us of the strategic importance of charismatic tasks and gifts. If prophecy is wholly dead, if that goodly fellowship has finally ended, then so has effective contact with the Eternal. Then we would be forced to concede victory to the "flat-earthers—[those] thinkers who reduce every vertical to a horizontal, all language to the literal meaning of words, all relation with God to a relation with men."[4] Luke warns us that unless the vocation of Jesus continues, we would be left with accepting the utter futility of his ministry and the utter emptiness of his promise of a baptism with Holy Spirit and fire. If the demise of prophecy is a necessary casualty of historical change, then the Christian gospel is also a casualty.

It may, of course, be true that Luke's belief in the necessity of a charismatic succession within the church must be modified. The church has at various periods suffered much from an excess of this spiritual gift; not seldom has it been driven to madness and broken into fragments by the frenzy of its prophets. One might draw up an extensive list of epochs when the church survived such frenzy only after prolonged torment—the Pauline congregation in Corinth, the outburst of Montanism in the second century, the enthusiastic sects of the sixteenth century, the revivalistic orgies on the American frontier, and the cultural vandalism of Jesus freaks in our own day. In not all cases does Spirit-possession entitle recipients to good standing in the Lucan roster of prophets. Nor does the opposition to Pentecostal excesses invariably bespeak the backlash of institutional defensiveness. Our question—does the prophetic succession continue?—may elicit both negative and positive answers, and both may be wrong. If that succession does continue, it brings with it the assurance of conflict between false prophets and true. On the other hand, we do not escape the issue by denying the existence of prophecy, nor by supercilious disdain for the ecstatic phenomena which so disrupt the bland gentility of traditional services of worship.

It may be true that in this regard Luke is a bad guide for our day. The Pauline or Johannine traditions may be better. I have not chosen Luke because of personal attraction to his theology, but simply because he is *there*. Though as a thinker he is regarded by many scholars as inferior to Paul and John, he remains a major writer in the sacred canon; it is a salutary rule that each of us should listen with special alertness to writings that are not our favorites. To be content with our own canon within the canon is very dubious testimony to faith in Scripture; only by listening to the whole of Scripture do we indicate its authority for us, a principle which has been ably defended by Professor B.S.Childs.[5]

Yet in defending the canon, we must recognize that its authority has often been wrongly substituted for the authority of living prophets. In fact, the fears of unfettered prophecy probably speeded the processes of canonization in the early centuries, for written documents can protect readers from the awful dilemmas posed by the unpredictable freedoms of charismatic leadership. Fundamentalist phobias find written dogmas highly superior to spoken prophecies, and this is true whether one is thinking of a fundamentalism of doctrine, of ritual, of office, or of cultural conservatism. Even the Westminster Confession expressed strong preferences for written forms of revelation, and discouraged any reliance on charismatic inspiration (pars. 6–10). We can hardly deny that this reliance on written Scripture has resulted in the gradual atrophy of the prophetic consciousness. Its world view evaporates, its language dies, and the expectation of prophetic guidance vanishes.

It is at this very point that we must be thankful that the church included Luke's twin volumes within its sacred canon, because these volumes register a vigorous protest against such conservative tendencies. By that action, the church voted for a conception of its own history in which prophetic reinterpretations of Scripture should be gladly accepted as signs of God's continued guidance. As we have seen, such reinterpretations accompanied every forward step from the message of Jesus in Luke 4 to the message of Paul in Acts 28.

Luke was no biblicist, no fundamentalist; he had too vivid a sense of the perennial struggle between scribe and prophet, too acute a memory of how the Spirit chooses to be active where least expected. Of course he accepted the authority of the Law and the Prophets, but he knew that the appeal to that authority was a favorite ploy of Satan. Only the gift of true prophecy could lead to a reinterpretation of those documents which would restore their vitality as the voice of God in the day of decision. Moses, the author of the Law, had himself been a prophet who continued to confront the covenant people from the future as well as from the past. In Luke's day, reliance on the covenants with Abraham, Moses, David, and Isaiah had become the cover up for treason against God, and authentic prophets had to demolish that cover. Without the work of such rebels there would have been no Christian Scripture to canonize. By including Luke-Acts within the canon, the early church declared authoritative this prophetic attitude toward Scripture and accepted living Christian prophets as continuing guides in the *re*interpretation of the written covenants. By canonizing the Book of Acts the church accepted Pentecostal gifts as authentic fulfillment of the vocations of the apostles, Jesus, John, Isaiah, and Moses. In doing this, the early church warned later churches against any appeal to the canon which would substitute frozen for molten revelation, and invited them to listen to contemporary prophets as interpreters of written Scripture. So we return to the question whether this author can help us determine if prophecy is still alive today.

To answer that question we should recall Luke's conception of the nuclear features of that vocation. Prophecy lives and can live only where a community accepts "the absolutely primordial experience of revelation" (K. Rahner). Such an experience presupposes an acute awareness of the presence of a living God as the prime determiner of the community's destiny. Presupposed also is the firm expectation that this God is active everywhere and always, and that he is bound to his own people by a covenant that embraces their total fund of memories and hopes. Bound thus to the community, this God perennially takes the initiative in speaking to it through specially selected agents. This God is constantly doing new things, but apart from his intentional disclosure, the import of such things remains hidden from men. The revealed word of God becomes the touchstone of the truth, so the prophet becomes the eyes and the head of this community, with the gift of second sight and second hearing, which enables him to convey messages from the divine world not accessible to other men. The community, in turn, comes alive when it recognizes the power of God in signs wrought by the prophets and so discerns His word in their words as to repent and believe.

At almost every point such a reliance on revelation is alien to the consciousness of the Christian community today. In fact, the character and boundaries of that community are too nebulous and too vague to permit a clear sense of any distinctive identity, origin, duty, or destiny. Its awareness of God is too amorphous and flickering to provide it with steady sustenance or with dependable contact with ultimate reality. And where this is true it is inevitable that reports of God's acting and speaking through chosen spokesmen become quite incredible, and expressions like the *fear of God* or the *love of God* simply echo the hollowness of the heart.

Or consider other aspects of the prophetic task. The prophet is a herald, a broadcaster of news which is intended to place both the prophet and his people under the constraint of urgent response. What can that signify when there is no one who listens to the prophet, when his language has ceased to carry meaning? The prophet is a *re*interpreter of Scripture, showing how it applies in unexpected ways to current happenings. What if this Scripture has actually ceased to be Scripture, having lost its power to map the world of thought and action in which the community lives? The prophet in the New Testament was accompanied by an astonishing array of signs and wonders, by healings and exorcisms, by miraculous knowledge and power. Which of our congregations would be prepared for such a sign next Sunday morning, prepared either to understand or to tolerate it? In Luke's view the succession of prophets was united above all by the fact of rejection, suffering, and martyrdom—from Abel to Zechariah. A prophet's mission could not be accomplished otherwise! Can anyone contend that such a notion, as applied to contemporary prophets, is deeply lodged in the consciousness of our churches and accepted either as a necessary criterion of the best preaching or accepted as an essential component in the definition of church membership?

Another characteristic of authentic prophecy was its ability to address the immediate situation of the community as a whole, including the whole range of political and economic conditions and
emergencies. Because the poverty and captivity which Jesus addressed in Nazareth had included both internal and external dereliction, both political and religious leaders became alarmed at his activity. Typically, then, the prophet called not for the avoidance of
political options, but for a line of action which created new align-
ments of all human relationships, inclusive of the political, the
economic and the religious.[6] Where is such a demand being presented or being obeyed today? Christian spokesmen are increasingly
restricted to a narrow wavelength of inner pieties, and thus more
social reformers are being produced by civil religion, as defined by
Robert Bellah,[7] than revealer-prophets by the churches in their
capacity as the people of God.

The totality and radicality of the prophets' demand was grounded
in their announcement of a new world coming. Those who responded to John were set in motion by fear of the coming wrath;
those who followed Jesus were impelled by a sense of the fullness of
the time and the nearness of the kingdom; those who obeyed the
apostles had come to terms with the signs of a new age of the Spirit.
With each change in the time consciousness came far-reaching
changes in every other area of thought. The past came to be dominated by new memories, the future by new hopes, the present by a
new covenant in the death and resurrection of the prophet like
Moses, a covenant renewed in baptism, the common meal, and daily
prayers. Prophecy replaced the sense of time as a calendar line by the
sense of time as a plumb line and a power line. "Dying, behold we
live" (II Cor. 6:9). Every witness to Christ became the witness to an
encounter with a new age, with light-saving time. But if this trans-
formation in the sense of time be taken as measure of the prophetic
vocation today, where in the world would we find it? It is entirely
possible that, like other epochs in the history of both Israel and the
church, ours is a period when we must wait in patience for some
future outburst of prophecy. Our consciousness, our vocabulary, our
world view has been de-propheticized. John Taylor's assertion helps

us to see the contrast between prophetic and contemporary attitudes toward time: "The prophets play fast and loose with time, to the great confusion of us who live by clock and calendar."[8] By contrast, we play fast and loose with the Eternal, to the great confusion of those who live by faith, hope and love.

So, as we review those features which were to Luke essential marks of Christian prophecy, we are forced to admit the dearth of those features in American churches. That dearth becomes even more striking when we recall Luke's emphasis upon the necessary role in the prophetic vocation of impotence, poverty, and dereliction. We recall how Jesus addressed his redemptive mission to penitent lepers and demon-captured sinners, how his powers as physician stemmed from his refusal to heal himself, how slow were his apprentices to learn to share the ignominy of the cross, and how necessary was the messianic suffering as prelude to the messianic glory. We are quite blind to the central message of Luke unless we take seriously his insistence that a person could win credibility as a prophet only by sharing in that suffering, and that a person could become a believer only by a life of imitation:

> Only at one point, only on one subject—but then consistently, universally—is Jesus our example: in his cross. . . . The believer's cross must be, like his Lord's, the price of his social non-conformity. It is not, like sickness and catastrophe, an inexplicable, unpredictable suffering; it is the end of a path freely chosen after counting the cost.[9]

It is the tremendous distance between such an understanding of the prophetic vocation and the mentality of American churches which justifies almost unlimited skepticism concerning the existence today of the same vocation. One could almost, in a fantasy of the imagination, suppose that Luke designed the stories of Peter in the Gospel to match the treasons of latter-day churches: treasons in dread of poverty and weakness, in ambition for personal status, in hostility toward enemies, in reliance on the security of swords, and in building chapels for ancient heroes in preference to obeying them.

We should not be content, however, with so bleak a picture. In painting it, we may be relying too heavily on current moods of despondency and on a wooden concept of prophecy. We must not underestimate the flexibility and variety in Luke's notion of charismatic gifts. That variety frees us from looking for precise correspondences between some biblical hero and a modern counterpart. Because his analogical thinking was so mobile we cannot turn his stories into dogmatic formulas or pious stereotypes. To him the word of God released diverse kinds of ministry and even more diverse modes of speech. That speech utilized virtually all grammatical styles: "exhortations, admonitions, denunciations, predictions, prayers, poetry, songs of praise, dogmatic expositions, etc."[10] All kinds of visions, dreams, and daily events could be employed. Characteristically, verbs of action were preferred over more static nouns. For instance, the noun for good news appears twice, the verb for proclaiming that news some twenty-five times. Consequently, he relied more on stories than on abstract concepts; his visions of heaven were more decisive than formal doctrines of God, his encounters with Christ more significant than creedal formulas. Stories of prophetic work remained open-ended, open toward new visions of God, open toward the future fulfillment of past promises, open toward God's selection of new audiences. Luke did not limit charismatic gifts to a carefully selected *Who's Who,* but included many anonymous men and women. Nor did he confine the gifts to a group of professionals, but included the entire community within the realm of the Spirit's guidance. He believed firmly in the "prophethood" of all believers as well as in a succession of revealers and healers.

Bearing in mind this diversity in charismatic roles, we may return to the basic question of whether we can discern within today's churches any signs of the prophetic succession. In pondering that question we immediately face another contrast between Luke's situation and our own. In his day a single person often served as the recipient of many gifts; he was called to reveal, to heal, to exorcise demons, to interpret Scripture, and the like. By contrast, we expect these various gifts to operate through various groups, each of which has been professionalized. To one professional group we assign the interpretation of Scripture; to another the tasks of preaching to "the faithful"; to still other groups the work of healing and counseling. To that vast, and usually passive, audience of nonprofessional church members there is assigned the task of supporting the cast of professionals. They are expected to listen to this cast, and for this listening the Spirit needs to provide no special gift. Because of this division of functions, we will suggest answers to the question in terms of self-examination by each of three groups: the priest-preachers, the responsible laity, and the scribal interpreters of Scripture.

Ministers can hardly avoid asking, at least on occasion, what connections link their professional work to the prophets, as pictured by Luke. To be sure, the services of ordination in most denominations assert the reality of a direct line of descent. Prayers on those occasions often call on God to give this man or woman the spirit of prophecy. Usually hymns are chosen to celebrate such a gift:

> Anoint them prophets. Make their ears attent
> To thy divinest speech; their hearts awake
> To human need; their lips make eloquent
> To assure the right, and every evil break."[11]

For many of us the recollection of those prayers and hymns at our own ordination evokes the sadness of diminished expectations and forgotten promises. Far from seeing ourselves as legitimate descendants of the prophets, we are more likely to charge ourselves with the guilt of standing among those who persecute them. Our vocational demoralization stems in some degree from the convergence of three facts. (1) Of all contemporary professions ours has been assigned the greatest responsibility for serving as heir to biblical prophecy. (2) Virtually no one in our own day, whether inside or outside our own parishes, actually responds to our work as if we were prophetic revealers of God's mysteries. (3) It has been so long since we ourselves have been made conscious of God's specific demand on us to disclose his will to a specific audience that this sense of vocation has virtually atrophied within our own hearts. For most of us these are simply facts to be candidly admitted. Whether or not we deplore them, it remains true that we ourselves see little intrinsic connection between the contemporary clerical profession and the ancient prophetic vocation. Indeed we are more inclined to stress an intrinsic incompatibility between the two, for nothing seems better designed to prevent the recurrence of prophecy than the professional clergy. Of this fact, the agonies of the celebrant in Leonard Bernstein's "Mass" is a poignant reminder. [12]

In saying this I do not want to add to the masochistic tendencies so dominant among us. But honest appraisals may be a sign of health, not of pathological self-flagellation. It may be true that God has neither called a particular person to be a prophet nor given him such a distinctive charisma, and without such divine initiative it would be dishonest and presumptuous to speak of prophecy. Moreover, Luke keeps reminding us that God calls only when he has a specific message to convey to a specific audience in an immediate situation. It may well be true that God has not chosen us to relay such a message. It may well be true that a given congregation is not akin to the audience to which God sent John or Jesus or Peter. It may well be true that the earlier message through them cannot be honestly reinterpreted as conveying his present demand and promise to the First Church of Megalopolis. Among many other temptations, ministers must beware of the temptation to force artificial applications of ancient riddles to modern dilemmas. The wind continues to blow where it chooses. The prophetic vocation is always perverted when men twist their self-image to conform to an inherited stereotype in the impatient desire to salve their consciences or to give their congregation a synthetic religious experience. The gift of prophecy cannot be professionalized, and woe to any person or church which tries to institutionalize it. The least of the prophets is greater than the greatest of clergymen.

Having said this, however, I want to develop another possibility: Luke may help us to recognize prophetic gifts in operation but unnoticed by us, and thus he may show us unsuspected continuities between prophets then and now. If we take seriously the criteria we have singled out, they may help us to detect insignificant events which match those criteria better than we have supposed. Let me be more specific.

In virtually every service of Christian worship the congregation hears a call to repent, joins in a verbal confession of sins, and receives the spoken assurance of forgiveness. The power of ritual to anesthetize is, of course, so strong that this moment may be nothing more than a perfunctory bowing before an extinct totem. But assume that on some rare occasion this moment comes alive, that it serves to crystallize a congregation's memories and hopes in a luminous experience of encounter with God's plumb line. When one selects this occasion and places it under the microscope of honest analysis, he may find within it the essentials of prophetic experience. If the act of repentance is real, it is drastic; if it is drastic, a plenitude of apocalyptic forces lies latent within it: the invasive presence of an ultimate mystery and majesty, the call to repent (not unlike John's), the irrepressible cry for forgiveness and healing (not unlike the lepers and the demon-ridden prisoners in the Gospels), the announcement of God's blessing (not unlike the blasphemy of which Jesus was accused), the miraculous cleansing and the gift of new energies, the closing of doors on years of captivity and the opening of doors on the year of Jubilee. This moment, which passes so briefly in the liturgy, may refract the entire course of a community's life. When that happens, it becomes an authentic capsule of prophetic renewal, all the more significant because of its apparent insignificance as a mumbo jumbo of mingled sounds. A professional clergyman who has become God's instrument in such a time should not too hastily deny all participation in the prophetic succession. To some degree he has become both seer and exorcist.

Or we may consider that rare instant when one person is privileged to discern the secrets of another's heart. It may not happen for years; yet when it does happen, it may betoken the presence of the prophetic charisma. The opening of doors into heaven often coincided in the biblical lexicon with the opening of doors into another's heart. Judged by this standard, the gift of prophecy is not entirely absent in our day, though resistance to such disclosures is as strong as ever, and all the conventional masks and alibis are readily available. Even so, on occasion the rusty hinges do swing open and a stranger's eyes may be accorded a fleeting glimpse of another's hidden anguish and heroism. Sometimes the stranger is a clergyman; sometimes it is his faith and his victory over self-interest that have qualified him for this mysterious, if momentary, power to exorcise demons from a tormented ego. Wounded himself, he is given the power of healing. With the gift may come an overwhelming realization of the joy in heaven that welcomes each sinner who repents, each leper who is cleansed. Though he remains sceptical of such signs, he may well see in what has happened nothing less than the moving of mountains, the defeat of abysmal forces, the de-demonization of existence. This event and his awareness of its implications may link him more closely than he dreams to the vocation of ancient seers and exorcists. When we begin to subject ordinary situations to X-ray photographs that disclose the "principalities and powers" at work within them, we may see the truth of Jacques Ellul's observation that, from the standpoint of Christian hope, every moment of man's life is apocalyptic. And when that is true, every moment becomes the occasion for second sight and second hearing, that is, a moment when God calls a prophet to announce the dawn of a new day.

I have left unmentioned until now that task of the clergyman which would presumably be mentioned first among the links in the chain which connects him to biblical prophecy: the act of preaching. Why have I shied away from it? One reason is that in my judgment few things so clearly mark the distance between *us* and *them* as our sermons. What we call preaching, and especially what we call prophetic preaching, provides all the evidence needed to convict us of betrayals innumerable and of guilt unspeakable. For Luke preaching was the act of a prophet disclosing the will of heaven; to claim that of today's preaching should provoke derisive laughter. Every time we read the New Testament we condemn ourselves anew. Yet there is something more to be said even in this day of hard-nosed realism and professional masochism.

On the one hand, if we were to place under the scriptural X-ray the struggles of some men who have left the priesthood, we might discern in them some of the marks of prophecy: the demand for a penetrating honesty; the awareness of what preaching should mean, making intolerable what preaching has come to mean; the birth of courage and freedom to leave a form of personal captivity that has become demon-ridden. Men who have stayed in the priesthood may need to hear as the word of prophecy the testimonies given by the dramatic departure of some of their colleagues.

On the other hand, signs of prophecy may also be discerned in the quiet testimony of men who have decided to stay, fully aware of all the reasons for leaving. In that struggle, they, too, may have received gifts of freedom, courage, and serenity not their own. Their decision may be grounded in new humilities and honesties, disclosing afresh the mystery and majesty of God's presence. The struggles of both those who have left and those who have remained may thus show us that modern preaching *should* continue the tradition of ancient prophecy even though it usually betrays that tradition; the issue to be determined is not the status of the profession but the calling of God and the response of the human heart.

It remains true, of course, that the prophetic anointing always includes a commission to preach. Yet each generation develops its own stereotype of what that preaching entails, an image always compounded of both true and false components. Moreover, such stereotypes are usually more restrictive and inhibiting, less diverse and flexible, than the flood of charismata released in the early church. With his appreciation of diverse spiritual gifts, Luke can liberate us from our conventional images. He can restore to each the integrity of being faithful to his own gift, whatever it may be. He can make us more keenly aware that overwhelming importance belongs less to the prophet himself than to the One whose word is to be spoken and the audience whom he has designated. Such a message is by nature both eschatological and theological. The theology of the prophets was, after all, nothing if not their preaching.

When the word of God came to the prophets, it summoned them

to a shared vocation and gave them whatever gifts were needed to fulfill their assignments. But the Spirit not only supervised their signs and words, it also exerted power to command faith among the listeners or to arouse hostility, both responses being signs of the Lord's doing. Even the stoning or crucifixion of the messengers disclosed a hidden origin in the mysterious battles between Christ and "the power of darkness." From the very beginning the crowds were warned to take care of *how* they heard; if their hearing led to obedience, that was a response to the Spirit, made possible by the Spirit.

The modern congregation, therefore, may well examine itself, asking in what sense it is a lineal descendant of the ancient crowds, whether of those who came out to hear John or Jesus, or of those who were present at the first Pentecost. Does it discern any spiritual gifts within the context of its own responses to the prophetic words and signs? It is a long time, of course, since it was expected that every church member should exercise some gift of the Spirit. That was Luke's attitude, but he may have been guilty of romantic exaggeration. Our exaggeration may well point in the opposite direction, where any outburst of ecstasy would lead to congregational schism, since most members would react to such an outburst with incredulous suspicions and explosive animosity. There seems to be a dearth in the gift of listening that is an exact counterpart to the dearth in the gift of prophetic speaking. Often the laity welcomes the reduction of prophecy to the profession of preaching because this reduces their obligation to that of paying the preacher's salary. When no charismatic gifts are expected of them, they relish the relaxing of the constraint to obey. Small wonder that so many are frightened by any manifestation of Pentecostal gifts. Even less wonder that they are angered by calls for civil disobedience, for the repudiation of military force, or for an exodus from our own editions of Babylon. Their unbroken allegiance to Caesar and mammon, their captivity to custom and convention, these belie any claim to baptism by water and the Spirit. How ridiculous to expect them to discern God's plumb line testing the walls which they have built!

Yet even here something more must be said. It is not wholly insane to believe that Jesus continues to send his laborers, usually incognito, into various houses and towns, continuing the mission of the harvesters in Luke 10. Nor is it impossible to suppose that from time to time they receive such hospitality as is due to their commander. The forms for extending this hospitality are endlessly diverse. Some auditors may be impelled by the announcement of good news to become involved in radical political activities in which solidarity with the poor leads them to break away from the conventional Christian congregation. Others within the borders of that body will find their deafness penetrated by the reading of Scripture, so that hymns and prayers are renewed as channels of two-way conversations. It is not impossible for the Spirit to accomplish its goals through hoary customs and apparently moss-grown conventions. It is as difficult to trace the operations of the gift of listening as of the gift of speaking, or healing, or forgiving. The clues provided by Luke's story of Pentecost are worth using. He detected evidences of the listening gift in such phenomena as the following: baptism, the breaking of bread, fear of divine judgment, prayers for God's grace, glad and generous hearts, willingness to have all things in common, the praise of God, and not least devotion to the apostles' teaching and fellowship. One might search in America without success for a complete replica of that fellowship, but to deny any trace of such a community would in fact be to announce the total extinction of the twin gifts—prophetic utterance and prophetic discernment. And for that conclusion there is even less evidence.

Now let me invite professional interpreters of Scripture to the same kind of self-examination. How faithful have we been to the prophet Jesus in our interpretations of the prophetic vocation? For many years it has been the fashion to bewail the sketchiness of our knowledge of Jesus. There is obvious truth and modesty in such a confession. And yet I think our problem is quite the reverse. I think we know too much about him, too much that threatens our church and our world, too much that does not accord with our own academic manners and motivations, too much that would shake the foundations were we to listen to him. We are haunted not by what we don't know but by what we do.

Scribes will always, of course, encounter peculiar difficulties in dealing with the written records of ancient prophets. They have been assigned the task of interpreting those records; in fact, most Americans regard them as the Supreme Court in matters of scriptural interpretation (which unfriendly critics may compare with congressional authorization of lumbering companies to control logging in the national forests). One result of giving scribes such a monopoly was pointed out long ago by Albert Schweitzer: their quest for the historical Jesus ends in their seeing the face of a liberal Protestant at the bottom of a deep well. Yet even unfriendly critics must admit that this caricature is no longer accurate. The face which contemporary scribes see is no longer the face of a liberal Protestant, nor of a Roman Catholic, nor of a Greek Orthodox, nor even of a Christian. It is rather the face of a Jewish prophet set to go to Jerusalem. It is the face of "that strange man on his cross" (the title of the first series of Shaffer lectures by Richard Roberts),[13] and that face continues to haunt even the scribes.

As contemporary scribes, we should confess that we know altogether too much about the vocation of Jesus as prophetic successor to Moses and John—too much, that is, for our own comfort. How has that knowledge reached us? In part, to be sure, as a result of the slogging work of generations of scholars. But there is an even greater debt to another group. All knowledge of Jesus has in fact reached us by way of those prophets whom he called and trained to continue his own prophetic work. It was to them, as eyewitnesses and servants of the word, that Luke was indebted for the anecdotes which he relayed to Theophilus and to us. It may be that he was unduly optimistic when he anchored the witness of the twelve apostolic prophets to the baptism of John, but there is actually no evidence that he originated that idea. And there is every reason to suppose that Jesus himself called into existence this group of companions as

> a distinct and unique entity, a kind of brotherhood of healing preachers who divided their time between training by their founder and activity in the field.[14]

This group of companions shared a high vocation under God initiated by Jesus, a vocation requiring a strenuous occupation as preaching beggars and producing shared memories and anticipations. Their work provided the most natural occasions for recalling the prophecies of their Master.[15] The fact that they viewed their own mission as a continuation of his encouraged faithfulness to his legacy. If they were under no compulsion to freeze his teaching into verbal formulas, they were also under no impulse to substitute legendary vagaries for the constraints of obedience to him. It is their witness to his baptism, his ministry, his commands, his signs and wonders, his passion and victory, his continuing guidance and promise to return that confronts us in Luke's narrative. Ever since Luke, the church has relied upon this tradition for authentic clues to its own vocation. It is this continuous vocation that provides the necessary hermeneutical principle for interpreting the canon of Scripture. If we had greater respect for that vocation, we would have greater respect for that canon. We would thank God for the gift of his Spirit to the apostles and prophets who, in faithfulness to the prophet like Moses, now share with him in continual intercession for the church. Only gratitude for these prophets can qualify us to join with them in the *Te Deum:*

> The glorious company of the Apostles praise thee.
> The goodly fellowship of the Prophets praise thee.
> The noble army of Martyrs praise thee.

NOTES

CHAPTER 1

[1]J. V. Taylor, *The Go-Between God* (Philadelphia: Fortress, 1973), p. 224.

[2]Quoted by R. Bellah, in R.E. Richey and D.G. Jones, eds., *American Civil Religion* (New York: Harper & Row, 1974), p. 256.

[3]New York: Bantam, 1971, pp. 3ff.

[4]*Sickness Unto Death* (Princeton, N.J.: Princeton University, 1944), pp. 45–49.

[5]For fuller discussion of this point, see P.S. Minear, "The Transcendence of God and Biblical Hermeneutics," *Proceedings: Twenty-third Annual Convention, Catholic Theological Society* 23 (Washington, 1968): 1–19.

[6]Further explication of this problem may be found in P.S. Minear, "Christian Eschatology and Historical Methodology," in *Neutestamentliche Studien für R. Bultmann* (Berlin: Topelmann, 1957), pp. 15–23.

[7]Cited by J. Sittler, *Essays on Nature and Grace* (Philadelphia: Fortress, 1972), pp. 127–28.

[8]*Mist of Memory* (London: Vallentine, Mitchell & Co., 1973), p. 9.

[9]*Jesus Christ the Same* (New York: Abingdon-Cokesbury, 1940), p. 11.

[10]See P.S. Minear, "A Note on Luke 22:36," *Novum Testamentum* 7 (1964):128–34; idem, *Commands of Christ* (Nashville: Abingdon, 1972), pp. 178–90.

[11]See J.H. Yoder, *The Politics of Jesus* (Grand Rapids, Mich.: Eerdmans, 1972), chaps. 8 and 9.

[12]See P.S. Minear, "A Note on Luke 17:7–10," *Journal of Biblical Literature* 93 (1974): 82–87.

[13]*Paul's Intercessory Prayers* (New York: Cambridge University Press, 1974), p. 4.

[14]See P. S. Minear, *I Saw a New Earth* (Washington, D.C.: Corpus Books, 1968), pp. 228–46.

Chapter 2

[1]N. Sithole, *Obed Mutezo* (London: Oxford University, 1970), p. 27.

[2]*Kerygma and Myth,* trans. R.H. Fuller (London: S.P.C.K., 1953), pp. 2–4.

[3]Karl Barth, *The Word of God and the Word of Man* (Grand Rapids, Mich.: Zondervan, 1955), pp. 62f.

[4]For a general survey, see H. Traub, "Ouranos," in G. Kittel, ed., *Theological Dictionary of the New Testament,* vol. 5 (Grand Rapids, Mich.: Eerdmans, 1968), pp. 502ff.; also K. Barth, *Church Dogmatics,* III/3, pp. 374–440.

[5]Kittel, *TDNT,* 5:507f.

[6]*Otherworldliness and the New Testament* (New York: Harper & Row, 1954), p. 116.

[7]*Jesus As Seen by His Contemporaries* (Philadelphia: Westminster, 1973), pp. 110–20.

[8]Cf. J.A. Ernesti, *Elementary Principles of Interpretation,* trans. M. Stuart (Andover, 4th ed., 1842), pars. 83, 84.

[9]*Church Dogmatics,* III/3, p. 424.

[10]Ibid., p. 425.

[11]It is noteworthy that also in Luke 15:1–7 a direct correlation is asserted between the repentance of the sinner and joy in heaven.

[12]For recent defense of this reading, see A.R.C. Leaney, *The Gospel According to St. Luke* (New York: Harper & Row, 1958), pp. 59–68.

[13]See P.S. Minear, "Ontology and Ecclesiology in the Apocalypse," in *New Testament Studies* 13 (1966): 93–97; also in *Current Issues in New Testament Interpretation,* W. Klassen and G.F. Snyder, eds. (New York: Harper & Row, 1962), pp. 23–37.

[14]*Hope and the Future of Man,* E.H. Cousins, ed. (Philadelphia: Fortress, 1972), p. 71.

[15]"Ouranos," in Kittel, *TDNT,* 5:502ff.

[16]See P.S. Minear, "The Interpreter and the Nativity Stories," *Theology Today* 7 (1950): 358–75.

[17]"Luke's Use of the Birth Stories," in L.E. Keck and J.L. Martyn, eds., *Studies in Luke-Acts* (Nashville: Abingdon, 1966), pp. 111–30.

[18]For example, Martin Luther: "Not only was Christ in heaven while upon earth, but so also were the apostles, and so are we all, even while on earth and mortal, if we do but believe in Christ"; cited in E. Keller and M.-L. Keller, *Miracles in Dispute* (Philadelphia: Fortress, 1969), p. 209.

[19]See J.G. Davies, *He Ascended into Heaven* (New York: Association Press, 1958).

[20]See P.S. Minear, "Jesus' Audiences According to Luke," *Novum Testamentum* 16 (1974): 81–109.

[21]*Church Dogmatics,* III/3, p. 374.

Chapter 3

[1]Leonard Bernstein, "Mass."

[2]It would be unwise at this point to give a full analysis of the priority rating of different needs within a typical American community. One study of suburban

churches indicates that four things top almost every list: economic security, health, family morale, and social status. It is likely that there would be little contrast between a Christian and a non-Christian group in this regard. Also one may observe that there is little obvious intrinsic connection between these needs and the desperate cry of the psalmist, or between these needs and the God of the psalmist. See J. Ellul, *Hope in Time of Abandonment* (New York: Seabury, 1973), pp. viiif.

[3]See J. Jeremias, *New Testament Theology*, vol. 1 (London: S.C.M., 1971), pp. 103f.

[4]Ibid., pp. 112–13.

[5]It would divert us too far from our target to present a full analysis of Consciousness A. Granted the pluralism of forms taken by that consciousness, common to most of them would be the assumption that independence rather then dependence, even on divine help, is overwhelmingly desirable. People are measured by their competence, by their ability to cope with all situations. The following two citations reflect the antithetical attitude: "The mission of Jesus—and of his apostles—is directed first of all to those whom nobody wants because they are no good to anybody" (T.W. Manson, *The Servant-Messiah* [New York: Cambridge University, 1953], p. 60); "The Spirit does not give himself where our encounters are glib, masked, exchanges of second-hand thoughts. Our defences must be down . . ." (J.V. Taylor, *The Go-Between God* [Philadelphia: Fortress, 1973], p. 128).

[6]*The Servant-Messiah*, p. 60.

[7]J. Jeremias, *New Testament Theology*, 1:104.

[8]A. Fridrichsen was among the best interpreters as he traced the issue primarily to the modern "notion of reality" in which there is no room for perceiving how "the miraculous element exists with the origin of the church" (*The Problem of Miracle in Primitive Christianity* [Minneapolis: Augsburg, 1972], pp. 25, 58f.).

[9]See P.S. Minear, "Jesus' Audiences According to Luke," *Novum Testamentum* 16 (1974): 81–109.

[10]*Hope and the Future of Man*, E.H. Cousins, ed. (Philadelphia: Fortress, 1972), p. 91.

[11]*New Testament Theology*, 1:116.

[12]See P.S. Minear, "A Note on Luke 22:36," *Novum Testamentum* 7 (1964): 128–34.

[13]E. Keller and M.-L. Keller, *Miracles in Dispute* (Philadelphia: Fortress, 1969), p. 223.

[14]Ibid., p. 147.

[15]E. Bloch, as quoted in Keller, *Miracles in Dispute*, pp. 147f.

[16]See E.C. Hobbs, "Gospel Miracle Story and Modern Miracle Stories," *Anglican Theological Review*, Supplementary Series no. 3 (March 1974), pp. 125f.

CHAPTER 4

[1]J. Jeremias, *New Testament Theology*, vol. 1 (London: S.C.M., 1971), p. 151.

[2]K. Aland, ed., *Synopsis Quattuor Evangeliorum* (Stuttgart, Württembergische Bibelanstalt, 1964), p. 533.

[3]In the nature of the case, most prophetic utterances came orally during times of communal worship and would have left no written record. Occasionally, an early Christian prophet recalls earlier moments of revelation (e.g., Gal. 1:15; I Cor. 14:37; II Cor. 12:2–10). Only one prophet, speaking in the Spirit, relayed his messages in writing, the prophet John of the Apocalypse, and that was because he was imprisoned and unable to join his brothers at worship. There is debate, however, over whether we can accept John as typical of the prophets of his day, a debate in which I defend the affirmative side (see *I Saw a New Earth* [Washington, D.C.: Corpus Books, 1968]).

[4]"Luke-Acts, a Storm Center in Contemporary Scholarship," in L.E. Keck and J.L. Martyn, eds., *Studies in Luke-Acts* (Nashville: Abingdon, 1966), p. 22.

[5]For this interpretation of Acts 1:1, see I.H. Marshall, *Luke: Historian and Theologian* (London: Paternoster, 1970), p. 87; J.H.E. Hull, *The Holy Spirit in the Acts of the Apostles* (London: Lutterworth, 1967), p. 179f.

[6]"The Structure and Significance of Luke 24," in *Neutestamentliche Studien für R. Bultmann* (Berlin: Topelmann, 1957), pp. 165–86.

[7]"The Story of Abraham in Luke-Acts," in Keck and Martyn, *Studies in Luke-Acts,* p. 147.

[8]Readers are urged to evacuate from their minds many connotations of the word *prophet* which have accrued since biblical times. These connotations can only distort our efforts to recover the pattern of Luke's thinking. To help in such evacuation, I would suggest the following: J. Lindblom, *Prophecy in Ancient Israel* (London: Blackwell, 1962); H. A. Guy, *New Testament Prophecy* (London: Epworth, 1947); E. E. Ellis, "The Role of the Christian Prophet in Acts," in W. W. Gasque and R. P. Martin, eds., *Apostolic History and the Gospel* (London: Paternoster, 1970), pp. 55–67; N. Engelsen, "Glossalalia," Ph.D. dissertation, Yale, 1971; P. S. Minear, *I Saw a New Earth,* pp. 92–103.

[9]The image of go-between is effectively used to describe the activity of the Holy Spirit through the prophetic vocation by J. V. Taylor in *The Go-Between God* (Philadelphia: Fortress, 1973), chaps. 4 and 10.

[10]We should not exclude from the category of signs such symbolic gestures as Agabus' binding himself (Acts 21:11) or the apostolic demand for baptism. When God anointed a prophet with power (Acts 10:38), works and wonders followed which forced onlookers to ask "by what power" and "in whose name" these men and women were doing such things (Acts 2:19ff.; 3:12; 4:7; 5:12). Each sign produced a penumbra of astonishment, which, as M. Buber recognized, "destroys the security of the whole nexus of knowledge for him [the prophet] and explodes the fixity of the fields of experience named 'Nature' and 'History' " (*Moses* [New York: Harper & Row, 1958], p. 75f.). See also the discussion in E. Fackenheim, *God's Presence in History* (New York: Harper & Row, 1972), p. 12f. Or in a phrase of A. Codrescu, the prophet applies "techniques for sabotaging history with the aid of God."

[11]See J. Jeremias, *New Testament Theology,* 1:12–38. In all these varied tasks of community leadership, the prophets may be viewed as practitioners *par excellence* of situation ethics, if, as John Taylor has suggested, "a true situation ethic can be grounded on nothing but response to the unmediated reality of God" (*The Go-

Between God, p. 224). The prophet helped the congregation view each situation as the moment of divine judgment and the moment of divine promise, not as successive dates on a time line but as simultaneous dimensions of a relationship disclosed in worship.

[12]In Luke the term for witness, *martys,* denoted not so much a witness at a criminal trial, or a martyr who sacrificed his life for his faith, as one chosen by the Risen Lord to see, to tell, and to call God's people to repentance (see R. P. Casey, in F. J. Foakes Jackson and K. Lake, eds., *Beginnings of Christianity.* 5 vols. [London, 1920–33], 5:30–37). Each prophet's vocation included a built-in necessity: he must announce the fulfillment of Scripture, and that interpretation must be rejected by men (Lk. 4:16–30; 6:23; 11:47–51; 13:28, 33; Acts 7:52; see F. Schütz, *Der Leidende Christus* [Stuttgart: Kohlhammer, 1969], pp. 28f. 42f., 139).

[13]If Luke thought of any single event as the birthday of the church, it was this baptism rather than Pentecost. "The *laos* John prepared (1:17) is the ecclesia" (Walter Wink, *John the Baptist in the Gospel Tradition* [New York: Cambridge University, 1968], p. 71).

[14]See E. Fackenheim, *God's Presence in History,* pp. 16, 22.

[15]*John the Baptist in the Gospel Tradition,* p. 43.

[16]See P. S. Minear, "Jesus' Audiences According to Luke," *Novum Testamentum* 16 (1974): 81–109.

[17]*John the Baptist in the Gospel Tradition,* pp. 42f.

[18]Ibid., p. 75.

[19]Ibid., pp. 43f.

[20]See R. E. Brown, "Jesus and Elisha," *Perspective* 12 (1971): 85–104.

[21]W. H. Brownlee, "John the Baptist in the New Light of Ancient Scrolls," *Interpretation* 9 (1955): 75.

[22]J. Jeremias, *New Testament Theology,* 1:130.

[23]Ibid., p. 122.

[24]*The Servant-Messiah* (New York: Cambridge University, 1953), p. 38.

[25]See P. S. Minear, "The Interpreter and the Nativity Stories," *Theology Today* 7 (1950): 358–75.

[26]*The Servant-Messiah,* p. 49.

[27]Readers will find new implications in Luke's two volumes when they take the promises of God to Zecharias and Elizabeth in chapter 1 as an introduction to both volumes and when they read Acts as well as the Gospel as a fulfillment of John's prophecy.

CHAPTER 5

[1]E. Keller and M.-L. Keller, *Miracles in Dsipute* (Philadelphia: Fortress, 1968), p. 222.

[2]*The Christology of the New Testament* (Philadelphia: Westminster, 1959), pp. 13, 44–49; also see C.F.D. Moule, "The Christology of Acts," in L.E. Keck and J.L. Martyn, eds., *Studies in Luke-Acts* (Nashville: Abingdon, 1966), pp. 159–85.

[3]*The Death of Christ* (Nashville: Abingdon, 1958), p. 114.

[4]*The Prophet-King* (Leiden: Brill, 1967).

[5]See F. Schütz, *Der Leidende Christus* (Stuttgart: Kohlhammer, 1969), pp. 34f.

[6]Ibid., p. 83.

[7]See H.M. Teeple, *The Mosaic Eschatological Prophet* (Philadelphia: Society of Biblical Literature, 1957).

[8]"The Central Section of St. Luke's Gospel," in D.E. Nineham, ed., *Studies in the Gospels* (Oxford: Blackwell, 1955), p. 50.

[9]Other Christian authors were also familiar with the Mosaic analogy. It plays a significant role in the thought of the Gospel of John and the Epistle to the Hebrews; it is presupposed in the traditions incorporated in Mark and Matthew; there are brief allusions in the epistles of Paul and in the Apocalypse. Such wide usage reflects a general acceptance of the idiom among first-century churches, although there is no visible effort to standardize the meanings. See E. Boismard, "Jésus, le Prophète par excellence, d'après Jean 10, 34–39," in J. Gnilka, ed., *Neues Testament und Kirche* (Freiburg: Herder, 1974), pp. 160ff.

[10]Keller, *Miracles in Dispute,* pp. 125f.

[11]See P.S. Minear, "The Interpreter and the Nativity Stories," *Theology Today* 7 (1950): 358–75.

CHAPTER 6

[1]J. Ellul, *The Presence of the Kingdom* (New York: Seabury, 1967), p. 50.

[2]"The Role of the Christian Prophet in Acts," in W.W. Gasque and R.P. Martin, eds., *Apostolic History and the Gospel* (London: Paternoster, 1970), pp. 63f.; see also H.A. Guy, *New Testament Prophecy* (London: Epworth, 1947), p. 115.

[3]E.E. Ellis, ibid.

[4]See E.E. Ellis, *The Gospel of Luke,* New Century Bible Series (London: Nelson, 1966), pp. 170f. Professor Ellis presents cogent evidence that in 11:49–51 Luke had in mind Christian prophets and that Zechariah was a Christian who had been murdered in the temple courts about 67 A.D. See also G. Klein, "Die Verfolgung der Apostel, Lk. 11:49," in H. Baltensweiler and B. Reicke, *Neues Testament und Geschichte* (Zurich: Theologische Verlag, 1972), pp. 113–124.

[5]The story should be compared to Deuteronomy 18:15, 18 and Exodus 24. See E. Schweizer, *The Good News According to Mark* (Richmond: John Knox, 1970), pp. 181f.

[6]See H.C. Kee, "The Transfiguration in Mark: Epiphany or Apocalyptic Vision," in J. Reumann, ed., *Understanding the Sacred Text* (Valley Forge: Judson, 1972), p. 148.

[7]See P.S. Minear, "A Note on Luke 22:36," *Novum Testamentum* 7 (1964): 128–34.

[8]See "A Note on Luke 22:36."

[9]See J. Dupont, "La portée christologique de l'evangélisation des nations d'après Luc 24:47," in J. Gnilka, ed., *Neues Testament und Kirche* (Freiburg: Herder, 1974), pp. 125ff.

[10]*New Testament Theology,* vol. 1 (London: S.C.M., 1971), p. 235.

11*Type and History in Acts* (London: S.P.C.K., 1964), p. 224.

12*Language and Myth* (New York: Harper, 1946), p. 92.

13See K.H. Rengstorf, "The Election of Matthias," in W. Klassen and G.F. Snyder, eds., *Current Issues in New Testament Interpretation* (New York: Harper & Row, 1962), pp. 178–192.

14Ibid., p. 185.

15See P.S. Minear, "Jesus' Audiences According to Luke," See *Novum Testamentum* 16 (1974): 81–109.

16J. Fitzmyer, "Jewish Christianity in Acts in Light of the Qumran Scrolls," in L.E. Keck and J.L. Martyn, eds., *Studies in Luke-Acts* (Nashville: Abingdon, 1966), p. 244.

17I.H. Marshall, *Luke: Historian and Theologian* (London: Paternoster, 1970), p. 221.

18This feature is sharply expressed by a former Shaffer lecturer, C.K. Barrett: "To become a close disciple of Jesus is to receive a death sentence" (*The Sign of an Apostle* [London: Epworth, 1970], p. 78). In contrast to the flight of the Twelve in Gethsemane is the description in Acts 5:41.

19I.H. Marshall, *Luke: Historian and Theologian,* p. 201.

20See A. Ehrhardt, "The Construction and Purpose of the Acts of the Apostles," *Studia Theologica* 12 (1958):50 n.1.

21See H.A. Guy, *New Testament Prophecy,* pp. 98f.

22See J. Roloff, *Apostolat, Verkundigung, Kirche* (Gutersloh: Molin, 1965), pp. 169f.

23M.D. Goulder has provided a persuasive list of coincidences between Luke's picture of Paul as prophet and his picture of Jesus (*Type and History in Acts,* pp. 35f.).

24J.V. Taylor, *The Go-Between God* (Philadelphia: Fortress, 1973), p. 224.

CHAPTER 7

1J.L. Martyn, "Theological Education or Vocation," in J.Y. Holloway and W.D. Campbell, eds., *Callings* (New York: Paulist, 1974), pp. 251, 252, 259.

2See P.S. Minear, "Dear Theo: The Kerygmatic Intention and Claim of the Book of Acts," *Interpretation* 27 (1973): 131–50.

3See P.S. Minear, "Jesus' Audiences According to Luke," *Novum Testamentum* 16 (1974): 81–109.

4J.V. Taylor, *The Go-Between God* (Philadelphia: Fortress, 1973), p. 224.

5*Biblical Theology in Crisis* (Philadelphia: Westminster, 1970), chaps. 5–12.

6J.H. Yoder, *The Politics of Jesus* (Grand Rapids: Eerdmans, 1972), p. 23.

7In W.G. McLoughlin and R.N. Bellah, eds., *Religion in America* (Boston: Houghton Mifflin, 1968), pp. 5–20.

8*The Go-Between God,* p. 80.

9J.H. Yoder, *The Politics of Jesus,* p. 97.

10J. Lindblom, *Prophecy in Ancient Israel* (Philadelphia: Fortress, 1962), p. 36.

11D. Wortman, *Pilgrim Hymnal* (Boston: Pilgrim, 1962), 470.

[12]See also W.G. McLoughlin, "Is There a Third Force in Christendom?" in *Religion in America*.

[13]New York: Abingdon, 1934.

[14]E. Trocmè, *Jesus As Seen by His Contemporaries* (Philadelphia: Westminster, 1973), pp. 37f.

[15]Ibid., pp. 23f.

INDEX OF BIBLICAL REFERENCES

175